Enterprise Engagement For CEOs

The Little Blue Book
for People-Centric Capitalists

By
Bruce Bolger

Edited by Richard Kern

Published by the:
Enterprise Engagement Alliance
520 White Plains Rd., Suite 500
Tarrytown, NY 10591
(914) 591-7600, ext. 230
Bolger@TheEEA.org

ISBN: 978-0-9915843-5-2

Enterprise Engagement for CEOs

Table of Contents

Forward

"If organizational leaders worldwide had for all times practiced the principles outlined in this little blue book, there might never have been a "Little Red Book.""

By Dr. Gary Rhoads, Co-Founder, Enterprise Engagement Alliance *and Professor of Marketing and Entrepreneurship, Marriott Graduate School of Business at Brigham Young University in Salt Lake City and Chairman of Xvoyant, a fast-growing sales engagement company, and before that, founder of Allegiance, the first enterprise engagement company focused on connecting the voice of the customer to employees.*

With the right focus on the value of people, capitalism can create a virtuous circle of prosperity that surpasses the potential of any other system. *Enterprise Engagement for CEOs* is for a new generation of Purpose Leaders and proud capitalists who don't just *say* Human Capital is their organization's most important asset, they *know* it. By Human Capital, I mean not just employees or customers, but all stakeholders — distribution partners, vendors, communities, and investors. In the case of not-for-profits, this also means donors and volunteers, and in government, constituents, political donors and volunteers as well.

Enterprise Engagement for CEOs provides organization leaders or anyone who aspires to be one a logical, practical guide to a new strategic and systematic approach to people management that generates greater and more sustainable financial results than the prevailing process- and short-term focused management style. It also creates a better experience for all stakeholders and a healthier, more prosperous society, not to mention greater peace of mind for boards, management and investors.

Nothing about Artificial Intelligence or any other economic force will change the fundamental principle that Human Capital is an organization's most precious asset. One would hardly know it, though, based on the way most organizations are run, not only in the U.S. but throughout the world. Despite the many CEOs who say that people are their most important asset, many take or enable actions that hurt customers, employees, communities and other stakeholders in the name of short-term profit. Human Capital is not carried as an asset on any balance sheets except under the nebulous category of goodwill, and most organizations, public or private, disclose little information to anyone that would substantiate a serious commitment to Human Capital. In fact, surveys have shown that most CEOs do not even rank people among their top five assets.

The result? According to Gallup, less than 40% of employees are engaged in their work — a level unchanged in over a decade — at an estimated cost of hundreds of billions of dollars each year. Nearly two-thirds in a Monster.com survey said they get the blues at the start of the work week. As for consumers, overall satisfaction with product and service quality remains just above 70%, hovering in the same general range since the American Consumer Satisfaction Index was created in the last century. It's no wonder that a recent Gallup survey found that only about 33% of citizens are satisfied with "things in America," despite record employment.

Organizations arguably spend hundreds of billions each year to engage their stakeholders, whether in branding and marketing, leadership recruitment and coaching, motivational speakers, engagement surveys, communications in myriad forms, training, job design, innovation and collaboration, rewards and recognition and on and on. There are probably hundreds of useful business books on leadership, and an equal number of management training programs, and yet little has changed but the buzzwords.

The state of people management is analogous to the state of quality management in the 1980s, when U.S. and other organizations spent billions on quality control and new machinery and yet encountered stubbornly high defect rates exploited by the Japanese, who were adopting a proactive, integrated approach to quality management created in the West but largely ignored here. In 1987, ISO 9001 quality standards created a commonly accepted framework and nomenclature with a strategic and systematic approach that helped transform quality in manufacturing in the U.S. and elsewhere. Now, the principles of Enterprise Engagement embodied in the new ISO Annex SL and ISO

10018 Quality People Management standards can do the same for Human Capital management.

What makes this book required reading for any people-centric CEO?

The principles of Enterprise Engagement and ISO 10018 Quality People Management standards go beyond the already widely addressed issues of leadership skills to help CEOs apply the same strategic and systematic approach to people management today that ISO 9000 standards did for quality management in the 1990s. This easy-to-understand approach and completely voluntary ISO standards provide the principles and a roadmap from which any organization can benefit to achieve a greater return-on-investment from their current efforts to enhance their various stakeholders simply by using the proven strategic, systematic, integrated approach that transformed quality. The result is higher, more sustainable performance, a happier workforce and more satisfied customers and communities, not to mention investors.

Enterprise Engagement and ISO standards address the growing desire for human capitalism that benefits all stakeholders and society by demonstrating that a strategic and systematic focus on human capital offers a more successful and sustainable way to run an organization of any kind.

If organizations worldwide had always practiced the principles of this little blue book, there might never have been a Little Red Book.

Chapter 1

Why a CEO's Guide
to Enterprise Engagement?

This book is written for CEOs or senior management, Purpose Leaders who believe it's time to design and implement a strategic and systematic approach to achieving organizational goals by harmonizing the interests of all stakeholders towards the organization's purpose, goals, and objectives. Whether you're a CEO or part of the management team, this book provides everything your organization needs to get started on a more sustainable way to fulfill your brand promise, achieve your goals, enhance the experience of all stakeholders and, if yours is a public company, enhance your shareholder value.

How Engagement Drives Performance

Increase	Satisfaction and referrals.
Improve	Repeat business.
Increase	Sales.
Increase	Employee retention.
Improve	Community relations.
Maximize	Innovation and collaboration.

Fortunately, the same principles that apply to leading an entire organization also apply to any division or department within an organization, so that many of the basic principles and practices in this book can be used to enhance the performance of traditional engagement tactics such as coaching and learning, surveys, communications, learning, diversity and community, job design, incentives, recognition, loyalty, rewards and recognition, analytics and more.

What makes Enterprise Engagement new is its strategic and systematic approach to addressing the interests of all stakeholders. This integrated concept was first formalized by the Enterprise Engagement Alliance (EEA) in 2008 on the premise that organizations can achieve the most sustainable results if they foster the proactive and aligned involvement of all stakeholders—customers, employees, distribution partners, vendors, communities, investors and other key constituencies—and the EEA's Engaged Company Stock Index (ECSI) has borne this out by consistently outperforming the S&P 500 since its inception in 2012. The problem today at most organizations is that the CEO has no formal Human Capital strategy, defined culture, or Chief Engagement Officer in charge of creating a formal plan to define a common brand promise, culture, or values and to achieve goals and objectives in a unified fashion, rather than the current siloed, ad hoc and reactive approach.

In 2012, the International Organization for Standardization (ISO), acknowledged that it had overlooked a key factor in its standards: the role of people. The organization's well-known ISO 9001 standards helped transformed Quality Management in the 1990s, and ISO determined the same strategic and systematic approach can fix the people issue if the CEO assumes leadership. Over the last six years, ISO has published a dozen Human Capital. In 2015, ISO issued new Annex SL people management requirements applicable to 60 standards that now require CEOs at about 2 million ISO-certified companies to create and annually disclose a formal People Management strategy, and issued the ISO 10018 guidelines that provide the first standards and certification for Quality People Management. ISO recently issued the ISO 30414 guidelines on Human Capital Reporting for those organizations seeking a standardized way to audit and disclose information material to their stakeholders. Similarly, EPIC (Embankment Project for Inclusive Capitalism) recently issued eight metrics organizations can use to disclose human capital and sustainable management practices.

Now, the European Union has upped the ante on stakeholder management principles with its "anti-greenwashing Corporate Sustainability Reporting Directive which will require companies with over 250 emloyees, $44 million in sales, and other criteria will have to make detailed, audited and comparable disclosures in a central database of the risks and opportunities created for employees, customers, distribution and supply chain partners, communities, and the environment.

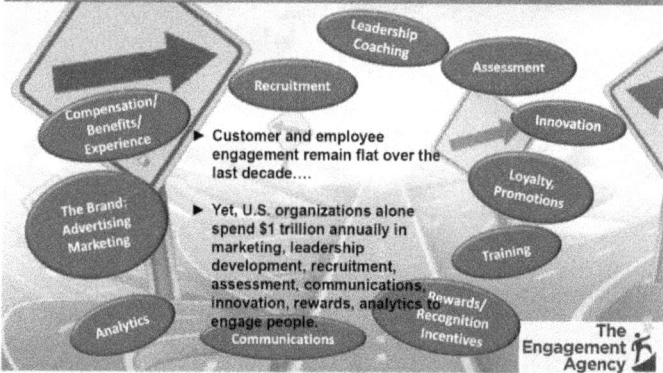

This book provides everything any organization needs to get started on the path to an Enterprise Engagement strategy. All your organization needs is a CEO ready to lead the way.

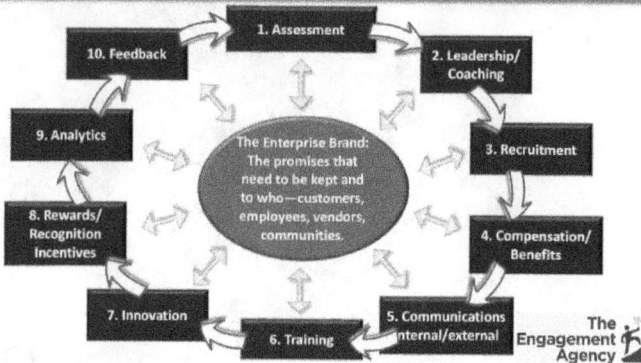

Chapter 2

The Enterprise Engagement Strategic and Tactical Implementation Process

To lead the implementation of a strategic and systematic approach to stakeholder engagement is a logical process that aligns already existing tools used in most organizations: branding, coaching, recruitment, communications, learning, community, innovation, loyalty, rewards and recognition, and analytics. The key is to achieve greater return on investment by integrating these processes to align with your organizational goals and by applying the latest best practices to process design and return-on-investment measurement.

Here is a summary of the key drivers of Enterprise Engagement and the corresponding business tactics that need to be integrated to create a formal Engagement Business Plan with a clear ROI.

THE FOUNDATIONS OF ENGAGEMENT

Based on dozens of research studies, here are the fundamental drivers of engagement that the framework is designed to address:

- A clear sense of mission or what the organization stands for
- Clear goals—where do we want this relationship to go?
- Emotional bonding—a sense of community
- Capability—are people able to do what is asked of them?
- Fun—a sense of humor
- Support—a sense of being valued and that someone human is inside
- Task value—a sense that what I'm doing has purpose
- Feedback—meaningful suggestions on how to improve.

The Foundations of Engagement

- A clear sense of mission and goals.
- Emotional bonding.
- Capability.
- Fun.
- Support.
- Task value.
- Feedback.

THE IMPLEMENTATION FRAMEWORK

This framework for implementing a strategic engagement process addresses the drivers of engagement outlined above to create an Engagement Business Plan that can be incorporated into an overall operating system with a measurable return-on-investment. (See Chapter 3, The Enterprise Engagement Operating System.")

Leadership: Clear goals, objectives and performance measurements.

Assessment: Engagement surveys; the nominal group technique to gain input from key groups.

A Coordinated Campaign: A business plan (often with a theme) with goals, strategies, tactics and measures, timed to an organization's planning cycle and targeted as appropriate to each audience.

Job Design: Cutting-edge organizations examine how they can craft jobs to make them more engaging and to enable people to share or relieve each other on tasks during certain periods.

Communication: An Intranet site or Engagement Portal that is the focal point for the campaign: a launch kit and/or poster or handout; ongoing use of available organizational media; meetings, emails, promotional products, etc. to distribute news, case studies, contributed content and highlight winners and best practices to get attention.

Learning: Incorporate the program into ongoing training and distributing periodic tests.

Collaboration and Innovation: Invite participants to contribute ideas, case studies, best practices, how-to articles, or whatever content can enhance the program.

Community and Diversity: What types of activities can an organization develop that foster a sense of camaraderie and empathy across the organization and attract talent and customers from the broadest possible spectrum?

Recruitment: Establishing a recruitment process in alignment with the organization's overall brand and values, as well as a candidate evaluation process aligned with that definition.

Recognition: Enable managers to recognize employees, and peers to recognize peers, for specified results, behaviors and actions.

Rewards: Use non-cash rewards to distinguish from compensation; use low-cost "treats" to broaden participation and fewer high level rewards to draw attention; encourage redemption at a company site where messages can be reinforced and where further assessment can occur.

Technology: You will be more able to manage and measure your program if you can house all of it on a single website that handles the content, communications, quizzes, rewards and recognition. If you cannot easily do this on your Intranet, there is now low-cost technology available for managing Engagement Portals, rewards, recognition and training.

Return-on-Investment: Try to assign a value to the results, behaviors, or actions being promoted; track results of ongoing engagement surveys and tests; look at website engagement metrics; track level of participation in recognition programs and surveys, etc. Ideally your organization uses no more than three to five measures and looks at both action measures as well as results/outcome to ensure a correlation between your plan and outcomes.

It goes without saying that unless full-time employees earn a living wage, they cannot possibly perform at their best, as they will be forced to earn money on the side or endure continued frustration. The topic of compensation is a field upon itself, but for the purposes of this book, compensation should be:

- Strategic and aligned with the ways people contribute value to the organization in financial and other relevant terms, with a justifiable range between the lowest and highest paid in publicly held organizations.
- Provide a clear path to growth for those who can add value over time.
- Enable everyone to benefit from their increased performance or value to the organization.
- Create opportunities for everyone to participate in success.

Sustainability Reports, covered in Chapter 4, provide organizations committed to people a means of touting their generous compensation and benefits to demonstrate their commitment.

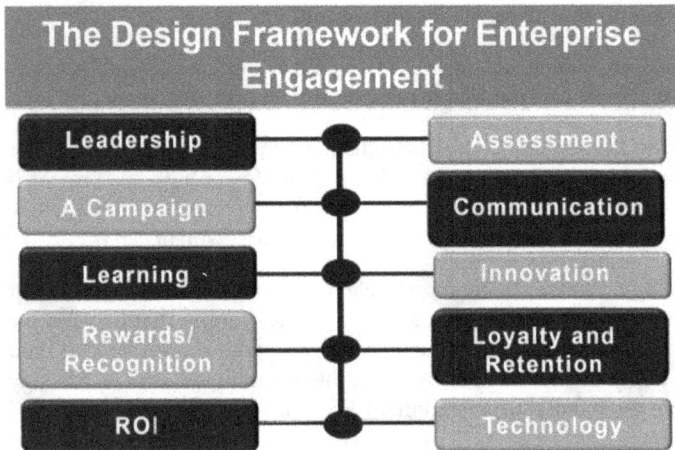

The Design Framework for Enterprise Engagement

Leadership	Assessment
A Campaign	Communication
Learning	Innovation
Rewards/ Recognition	Loyalty and Retention
ROI	Technology

Chapter 3

The Enterprise Engagement Operating System

The key premise of Enterprise Engagement and ISO 10018 quality people management and other human resources standards and guidelines is that organizations will achieve greater results if they apply a strategic, systematic, and proactive approach to stakeholder engagement rather than the prevalent ad hoc and reactive approach that is often divisive and inefficient.

The Enterprise Engagement Operating System (EEOS) is an "open source" management system for any size or type of organization developed to support Annex SL and ISO 10018 Quality People Management standards and requirements. EEOS provides to all organizations the strategic benefits of an organizational operating system that marries people with processes to achieve key goals. The open source approach means that we provide all the information organizations need to establish and implement their own internal Enterprise Engagement Operating System without being required to use an Enterprise Engagement Alliance-authorized Operating System advisor.

WHAT IS A MANAGEMENT OPERATING SYSTEM?

- **Definition:** A Management Operating System is designed to minimize CEO headaches and maximize efficiency and the experience for all stakeholders, from customers and distribution partners to employees, vendors and communities. As organizations grow in size and complexity, the risk of conflicting priorities, inefficiencies and siloed thinking expand exponentially. Aligning and focusing all the often-conflicting cultures, priorities, points of view and political camps can be daunting and aggravating. The

Enterprise Engagement Management Operating System provides the CEO and leadership team with a formal operating process to streamline the orderly development and achievement of organizational culture, goals and objectives, as well as a method for continually detecting and addressing challenges and opportunities along the way.

- **Key Benefits of an Enterprise Engagement Operating System:**

  Peace of mind. The process includes an annual plan with a clear roadmap, roles, responsibilities, milestones and scorecards, as well as carefully planned meetings with the right players and agenda to remain on track or address unexpected challenges and opportunities in a practical matter.

  Focus. It ensures that the organization keeps its eye on a common goal and priorities.

  Cost control. An effective EEOS process minimizes the chances of financial surprises.

  Alignment. The cross-functional component minimizes the chances for silos and infighting.

  Accountability. A disciplined approach ensures everyone knows their roles.

  More fun. Focused, disciplined and efficient processes help create consensus and productive camaraderie.

- **A Systematic Approach:** The EEOS provides a roadmap for effectively running any organization by creating a strategic and organized approach to the entire process of achieving success:

  o Developing the organizational brand and culture, goals and objectives
  o Mobilizing the people/teams/divisions needed to live the brand and culture and achieve the goals
  o Creating a simple system for continually monitoring progress
  o Identifying obstacles and opportunities
  o Developing and communicating solutions
  o Building communities
  o Rewarding and recognizing people based on accomplishments or positive actions
  o Measuring the results

o   Planning for the future.

- **Open-Source vs. Proprietary Systems:** A number of consulting firms and authors have developed effective but propriety solutions that require an organization to commit to a process based on the nomenclature, procedures and workbooks produced by a specific organization that can charge what the market will demand. If your organization uses one of those systems, it need not change as long as you make sure it addresses the human factor. If not, you can integrate into it your Enterprise Engagement plan. The materials used by the Enterprise Engagement Operating System are in the public domain. The Enterprise Engagement Alliance open-source model charges specifically for the content in the form of our *Enterprise Engagement: The Roadmap* guidebook; any workbook materials or tracking support software if desired; or for the training or advisory services required. This means that an organization can implement an open-source   process itself with minimal expense or hire as needed a trained EEOS facilitator. The greatest risk of failure comes not from the operating system selected, but from the failure to remain disciplined and to address both people and process issues.

WHAT IS AN EEOS?

If utilized, the Enterprise Engagement Operating System (EEOS) incorporates the procedures, processes, and people involved with an organizational plan--specifically, the process for the strategies, tactics and measures to achieve brand engagement and the goals and objectives through all people concerned. The EEOS links the Enterprise Engagement to day-to-day operations, goals and objectives. The goal is to make sure that the organization connects the dots between the strategies, the people and teams necessary to implement the plan and the processes necessary to track and measure results. This process also includes the methods for feeding back outcomes and other findings to the Planning Team and relevant people to regularly update the plan and improve performance over time.

The EEOS is unique in that it's based on an open source approach aligned with ISO Annex SL and ISO 10018 standards, which can be purchased from ISO for under $150 each, and on the content of *Enterprise Engagement: The Roadmap*, which can be purchased for $36. This means that no company is ever wedded to or dependent upon a specific expert and resource, and that the organization can be assured that its system will support ISO Annex SL and ISO 10018 standards and requirements should it seek ISO certification.

THE UNIQUE COMPONENTS OF THE EEOS

The Enterprise Engagement Operating System is unique in that it systematically connects people management processes with administrative processes so that all people are engaged in, empowered by and capable of doing precisely what they need to do to contribute to organizational success. EEOS addresses a frequent complaint with other operating systems by strategically addressing the human factor. The EEOS creates a simple system used at every level of the organization to make sure that everyone's activities align with the same organizational brand, values, goals and objectives, as well as internal and external customer and other stakeholder expectations. It can be used at both large and small organizations.

Ideally, the EEOS process ensures that people are emotionally engaged in the Enterprise Engagement Operating System.

The EEOS includes the following elements:

1. The Strategic Plan

2. Tactical Planning
   a. The appropriate timing and schedule for meetings and who's involved
   b. An execution plan

3. Personnel Planning
   a. A clear organizational chart with roles and responsibilities

4. A consensus-building/problem-solving process

5. Process management

6. Return-on-Investment Measurement, Evaluation and Feedback

   a. A scorecard

HIGH-LEVEL RESOURCE REQUIREMENTS OR DESIRABLES

1. **An EEOS Advisor.** A senior level executive trained in the Enterprise Engagement Operating System and/or an outside expert

EEOS consultant shepherds the entire process. He or she must understand the framework and the company, have strong communication and consensus-building skills and patience. This can also be handled by a capable internal executive with the authority to keep the process moving.

2. **A budget** for the planning process and the organization's management coaching, assessment, involvement & empowerment, marketing & communications, learning, community, rewards & recognition, data, analytics, return-on-investment measurement and feeding back the information to relevant parties.

3. **A Planning Spreadsheet** or other method of tracking timelines, project start/completion dates and roles and responsibilities. It should also break down goals and objectives into quarterly or more bite-size milestones or accomplishments.

4. **A Return-on-Investment** system that enables you to establish and track the qualitative and quantitative outcomes on an ongoing basis correlated against the plan to determine what worked and what didn't. This can include the use of an engagement survey.

5. **Optional Engagement Portal technology platform.** An organizational Engagement Portal technology can enable the sharing of all information based on the audience/stakeholders under a common theme that reinforces the goals, objectives and brand values to all audiences as appropriate. This includes a source for news and how-to information useful to each audience based on their relationship with the company; a platform for conducting surveys and knowledge tests, creating communities, a social wall or other platform for fostering and sharing suggestions; a system for rewarding and recognizing desired behaviors; and a means of feeding back information to relevant parties. The Enterprise Engagement portal platform can include an administrative function for management tracking of the strategic, tactical and individual business plans, meetings and outcomes.

Here are some more details on the components of the Enterprise Engagement Operating System.

Management Tools

The Enterprise Engagement Operating System requires only a few key workbook elements that can be kept in a binder or managed online:

1. Organization chart for roles and responsibilities.

2. Priority management worksheet to track three to five priorities at most for each operational time period.

3. Standard agenda for weekly 60- to 90-minute meetings, monthly half-day meetings, quarterly full-day meetings and one annual two-day meeting.

4. Communications platform to share information with all employees

Note: Most EEOS projects can be managed on a basic project management software such as Basecamp or Jira.

The Strategic Plan

- The EEOS process starts with having a strategic plan for the organization so that all objectives, activities and priorities can be established based on that plan.

- The strategic plan is created generally in a one- or two-day off-site meeting facilitated by the EEOS Advisor or the most objective and knowledgeable person possible.

- This meeting differs somewhat based on whether this is the first time the organization has used a formal Enterprise Engagement or related operating system, or whether this is an updated plan, and if it's part of a continuous improvement effort or change management process. The main difference is that the first meeting will probably take longer.

- A new plan may require more time because of the need to address all the issues below for the first time in a systematic way. The second year is easier because a revised plan is usually an update of what has been done in the past, unless the organization's leaders believe there's a need for radical change.

- To enhance consensus and the open sharing of solutions, the meeting can use the Nominal Group Technique—a round robin opinion/thought-gathering process (explained below).

Who: Heads of departments, and perhaps some employees

When: One to two months in advance of new fiscal year or other operational period.

Where: Held off-site to minimize distractions and often as part of team-building efforts to facilitate open, constructive communication.

What: An expert facilitator/advisor leads a full-day discussion in a retreat or off-site setting to:

- Establish or reconfirm the organization's brand, values and culture, goals and objectives, and critical management and marketing scorecards.
  - Try to keep goals focused on no more than three to five for the organization and about three for teams or individuals, or people will have trouble focusing.
  - There can be additional goals for sub-initiatives related to a specific team.

- A SWOT analysis to confirm strengths, weaknesses, opportunities and threats. This includes a review of investor, regulatory, or ISO standards, economic, trade, weather, or other factors that could affect the plan or disclosures of that plan and outcomes.

- An overall definition of key customer needs and preferences based on available research and evidence, weaknesses related to those needs and a review of what the organization can accomplish at the macro or micro level to address those needs or opportunities.

- A review of the overall strategic and tactical methods used to engage people in the plan and how that engagement will be measured.

- An updated organizational chart to confirm precisely who is accountable for each division/department or key activity related to the EEOS.

- A review of all current scorecard or other data, including customer or employee engagement measures.

- A review of potential silo or misalignment issues.

- Establishment of a brief weekly meeting between division heads to ensure lively and timely sharing of information related to developing, implementing and achieving the plan.

- Establishment of a Return-on-Investment Measurement, Evaluation and Feedback Plan, based on the objectives of the annual plan.

Tactical Planning

At large companies, it might be necessary to have each division repeat this process based on the strategic plan that comes out of the above annual process. This would be a carbon-copy of the above process.

The Nominal Group Technique Process

Here is a simple, useful means of ensuring your planning meetings obtain useful information from all involved and that they build consensus around a clear outcome.

- The facilitator reminds every one of the purpose of the meeting and the agenda.

- For each question, the facilitator goes around the table one by one. He or she can reverse order for each question if desired.

- People have a chance to speak but can pass if they wish.

- The facilitator or an assistant keeps notes on the screen or tablet on each idea, and ideas that might be duplicates are included unless a majority agree it's a duplicate.

- After all ideas are written up for all to review, the facilitator goes through each idea to make sure everyone agrees on the meaning and to remove any agreed-upon duplicates.

- Once that is complete, people vote for their top three ideas to identify the three or four most appropriate ideas or solutions.

Deliverable: The process is documented so that a complete report summarizing the findings with appropriate backup can be provided.

Process Management

This step ensures the connection between the Enterprise Engagement Business Plan, the Enterprise Engagement Operating System and desired outcomes and return-on-investment.

Resource requirements

- A qualified EEOS implementer.

- A spreadsheet or other process for managing tasks, dates, roles and responsibilities.

The key to connecting the dots is to employ or hire an EEOS Advisor/Implementer whose job it is to ensure that the plan is carried out. This person could be your company's Chief Engagement Officer or an executive advisor serving this capacity. (See Chapter 5, The Role of the Chief Engagement Officer.)

This process involves:

- Establishing and clarifying the essential processes in an organization and who needs to be trained in them.

- Ensuring that all team members are continually engaged in the process and updated with vital information.

- Creating a culture that focuses on serving the needs of external and internal customers.

- Ensuring the proper distribution of scorecard information.

- Scheduling of review meetings and preparation, including agenda-setting, arranging for facilitation, note-taking and, upon completion, preparation of the draft report for all to review prior to formal publication and sharing.

- Following up with division heads on their subsequent planning meeting schedule outcomes.

Return-on-Investment Measurement, Evaluation and Feedback

- This step involves implementation of the Return-on-Investment Plan developed in the Strategic Plan phase.

- The Advisor/Implementer is responsible for tracking the scorecard against the Return-on-Investment Scorecard on a regular basis established in the plan.

- The Return-on-Investment Scorecard can include:

  o **Quantitative measures.** Weighted, if desired, against their importance. A dollar value can be established, if desired, if the effort doesn't involve concrete revenue or costs.

- o **Qualitative measures.** Weighted, if desired, against their importance. A dollar value can be established, if desired, for the value of the qualitative achievements.

- The findings are shared with all leaders on the agreed-upon timetable (based on the pace of change in the organization) in advance of meetings to be discussed.

  - o The Implementer can come prepared with his/her own observations to start the meeting.

- After approval of the management team, the findings are shared with all relevant stakeholders with appropriate guidance and recommendations, if any. (See Chapter 5, The Role of the Chief Engagement Officer.)

- If the evaluation process turns up information relevant to a particular team or member, that information is shared in a personal meeting to discuss the implications and potential solutions.

Continuous Improvement

- All the information used during the feedback process is used by the strategic planning team when beginning the process going forward.

- The EEOS Advisor is responsible for providing a complete report on the outcome of the strategic and tactical efforts and key scorecard indicators, a discussion of which launches the agenda.

The 8 Principles of ISO 10018 Quality Management

1. Customer focus.
2. Leadership.
3. Involvement of people.
4. Process approach.
5. System approach to management.
6. Continuous improvement.
7. Factual approach to decision making.
8. Mutually beneficial supplier relationships.

Chapter 4

A Template for the Disclosure of Human Capital Practices and Measurements

There is a growing desire on the part of investors, regulators, customers, distribution partners, employees and communities to have a better understanding of the sustainable practices of the companies with which they engage. In fact, there are now multiple organizations that track the sustainable business practices of public and other companies, including the new JUST Capital Index that rates companies for their customer, employee, community, environmental and related practices. ISO (the International Organization for Standardization) has released guidelines for Human Capital Disclosures known as ISO 30414, applicable to almost any organization, that provide a detailed framework. An international organization of over 30 leading companies and investment firms formed a group known as EPIC (Embankment Project for Inclusive Capitalism) to develop disclosure recommendations for human capital and sustainable management practices.

As more investors require public companies to disclose human capital practices and outcomes, and with customers, employees and communities increasingly interested in how organizations treat people and the environment, CEOs face the challenge of determining what information is reasonable to disclose without giving up competitive advantages.

Here are recommendations from the Enterprise Engagement Alliance based on a distillation of ISO and other recommended disclosures that consider the need for simplicity and for avoiding the disclosure of competitive information. This guide as meant to provide organizations of any size with an ISO 10018-compliant framework for disclosing human capital investments, practices and outcomes to key stakeholders. Obviously, privately held and not-for-profit organizations would not face the same pressure as public companies to disclose quantitative information but can equally benefit by publishing an annual document demonstrating their commitment to each of their stakeholder groups.

While the Securities & Exchange Committee (SEC) is considering a petition to require public companies to disclose human capital investments and outcomes, action is not expected during this administration. But the current chairman, Jay Clayton, has outlined the criteria he feels are essential to such disclosures, as shared in a Feb. 11, 2019 meeting with investors. For the purposes of these recommendations, we are specifically addressing his stated criteria while incorporating the fundamentals of the far more thorough ISO 30414 disclosures.

Any organization can benefit from having a strategic and systematic approach to addressing the needs of all stakeholders, whether or not it is a public company, and all can benefit from disclosing such information, whether or not they are ISO certified, because investors, employees, customers, distribution partners, vendors and communities care about people as well. Therefore, these recommendations are based on addressing both the criteria considered essential by the SEC chair, as well as what would be reasonable for non-public companies to share.

The goal is to disclose information that is of use first to the organization in terms of effectively running its business from which can be extracted information that can be shared with key stakeholders without revealing competitive details about practices.

SUMMARY OF RECOMMENDATIONS

Ideally, disclosures include quantitative and qualitative information that can be compared by stakeholders to other organizations in terms of the quality of the information provided (see Final Recommendations below for details):

Quantitative

Readily available and comparable financial indicators of:

- Employee retention and productivity
- Customer retention and satisfaction
- Employee, customer and community well-being

Qualitative

The disclosures should include a written statement by the CEO outlining the organization's strategic and systematic plan for addressing the interests of all stakeholders with details on the various tactics used. As an example, see the disclosures made by the technology company SAP in its annual report. It includes extensive qualitative information on its management strategies related to addressing the needs of customers, employees, producers and all its stakeholders without disclosing details that would put it at a competitive disadvantage. Investors and other stakeholders can compare that report with the framework in the ISO standards or the EPIC or other recommendations for efficacy, as well as compare with other organizations in terms of quality of information provided.

THE BASIS OF OUR DISCLOSURE RECOMMENDATIONS

As stated, the specific recommendations below are based on the minutes of the Feb. 11, 2019 Investor Committee meeting and therefore address key issues raised by the SEC chair:

1. Materiality. Since the chairman has suggested a need to focus on disclosures that can provide leading, rather than lagging, indicators material to investors, there is only one criteria currently known to have a long-term impact on share prices: a high level of customer, employee and community engagement. Therefore, these recommendations will be limited specifically to quantitative and qualitative information related to the organization's ability to engage all key stakeholders in a systematic way.

Leading indicators of stock performance. There are now multiple independent studies, including the Alex Edmans London School of Business study referenced by the SEC, that have found a direct correlation between enterprise-wide engagement and share price performance. These include the Engaged Company Stock Index at TheEEA.org, a theoretical but easily auditable Exchange Traded Fund of about 45 companies with high levels of customer, employee and community engagement that has consistently outperformed the S&P

500 since its inception six years ago, and which is now over 30 percentage points ahead. Also, *Barron's* 100 Most Sustainable Companies, compiled by the Drucker Institute, has outperformed the S&P 500 for the second year since its inception. This new concept of sustainable management and investing led to the creation of the new JUST Capital ETF, launched in July 2018 by Goldman Sachs, which raised $215 million on its first day. Please note that while the London School of Business study indicates that employee engagement alone is enough to improve performance, the other two criteria also include the ability of the company to address interests of other stakeholders, i.e., customers and communities. JUST Capital is now tracking nearly 900 companies based on criteria including customer, employee, community engagement and job creation.

There are no other known leading indicators of stock price performance related to human capital than the ability to engage key stakeholders.

Implications. The SEC disclosure requirements should be narrowly focused on readily available objective financial and business information related to customer, employee and community engagement. Public and private organizations or investors and other stakeholders dedicated to Human Capital Management can use the ISO 30414 guidelines for further disclosure or evaluation purposes.

2. The impact of a CEO-led strategic and systematic approach to engagement. In 2012, ISO began a comprehensive process of completely updating its ISO 9001 Quality Management guidelines, ISO 45001 Safety guidelines and 58 other standards to address the human factor that ISO members determined they had overlooked in the original standards. ISO has since issued new Quality Management principles and Annex SL standards that require the CEO to take charge of a strategic and consistent process to "address the interests of all interested parties," including customers, distribution partners, employees, vendors, communities, regulators and shareholders. A new ISO 10018 Quality Management Certification is designed for any type of organization committed to implementing a CEO-led strategic and systematic approach to engaging all stakeholders.

ISO 30414 guidelines for Human Capital Reporting call for "a formal engagement strategy to support the proactive involvement of employees to consistently address the needs of external and internal customers that align activities related to leadership training, engagement assessment, communications, learning, innovation and collaboration, rewards and recognition, analytics and feedback."

Implications. It can be concluded that an organization with a CEO-led strategic and systematic tactical plan to engage all stakeholders has a potential advantage over organizations that do not. This information can be disclosed qualitatively through a statement from the company CEO outlining in broad terms the company's Human Capital strategy, known as a Sustainability or Integrated Report, including its overall strategic and a tactical plan to address all interested parties—customers, employees, distribution partners, communities, etc.—and a general overview of the tactics and outcomes. See the sustainability disclosures by SAP in its Annual Report for an example of such qualitative disclosures. Investors and other stakeholders can use readily available ISO guidelines to evaluate the validity of that statement.

3. Comparability. Many of the disclosures in the ISO 30414 guidelines are based on subjective information such as engagement surveys that cannot be easily standardized, especially across industries. Therefore, these recommendations for SEC disclosures are narrowly focused on readily available financial information and the CEO statement. The issue of industry-by-industry comparability raised by the chairman in the investor meeting is addressed by the ability for investors to compare the data by SIC (Standard Industrial Classification) codes, size of company and geographic location, as well as by using the ISO guidelines.

4. Flexibility. The chairman calls for standards that can change with circumstances. The EEA's disclosure recommendations focus on core leading indicators based on both empirical data and common sense. These recommendations are nuanced to address the primary motivations for non-compliance—i.e., the level of administrative burden and/or fear of disclosure of important competitive information. The specific recommendations below for SEC disclosure requirements are narrowly focused to include only readily available financial information, while being sensitive to a legitimate concern about releasing information that could put public companies at a competitive disadvantage with private concerns.

5. Efficiency. The disclosure requirements should be based on data that is either already available or, if not, a glaring indicator of an organization's failure to properly account for and manage human capital.

6. Responsibility. The requirements should be limited to financial information that most organizations need to run their businesses or to qualitative reporting by the CEO that enables investors or other stakeholders to make their own judgments as to the sincerity or efficacy of the Human Capital strategies and tactics. Requirements that give public companies a distinct disadvantage against private companies and upstarts, or burdensome new administration requirements, can and should be avoided.

7. The management perspective. The best regulations or standards help guide management toward successful practices rather than impede operations. Because of the strong correlation between stakeholder engagement, financial results and share price performance, requirements limited to disclosure of related data without putting public companies at a disadvantage by disclosing details on strategies and tactics likely will ensure a higher level of compliance.

RECOMMENDATIONS

The following information should already be accounted for at most companies, but does not require organizations to break out what they spend per tactic or number of customers, enabling them to protect sensitive competitive information:

Quantitative

- Number of full-time and salaried employees and independent contractors, compared with previous years.
- Overall payroll compared with previous years.
- Overall non-payroll expenses (incentives, recognition, benefits, training, excluding taxes), expressed in dollars or as a percentage of payroll.
- Employee retention (percentage retained year-to-year).
- Number of independent contractors (compared with previous years) and overall expenditures on independent contractors.
- Customer retention (percentage retained year-to-year).
- Overall expenditures in marketing and sales costs, and as a percentage of overall sales, compared with previous years.
- Number of reportable accidents/deaths compared with previous years.
- Expenditures in Corporate Social Responsibility, including comparisons with previous years.
- Number of lawsuits (by employee, customer, community), with year-over-year comparison.

Qualitative

Because a CEO-led strategic and systematic approach to engaging all interested parties are bedrock ISO principles, and because there are now voluntary ISO 30414 guidelines against which practices can be judged, we believe that a statement from the CEO in the filing can in fact be quite useful to knowledgeable investors and other stakeholders, especially those in a position to ask the right questions of CEOs in security analyst and other meetings with investors.

This report provides an explanation of the organization's brand, vision, values, and goals; its key stakeholders, and the specific processes it uses to address all their interests in order to foster their proactive involvement in success.

See the Whole Foods Annual Report from 2017 for an excellent example of a Human Capital report as well as the Sustainability or Integrated Reports from the CEOs of public companies featured in this book in Chapter 6.

In conclusion, these recommendations seek to directly address the requirements stated by the SEC chairman that weigh the concerns of all interested parties to provide information from which all stakeholders can benefit, including private, governmental and not-for-profit organizations.

Chapter 5

The Role of the Chief Engagement Officer

Ask anyone in management at large organizations about what frustrates them most, and one of the most common answers is silos—the walls that go up between different departments or divisions that lead to poor internal customer service, competition for resources, back-biting and worse. Silos not only cause frustration, they create inefficiencies that impede performance. There is now so much evidence that organizations that break down these barriers to address the interests of all stakeholders outperform their competitors that investors have taken notice: over $17 trillion in investment capital and multiple so-called ESG (Environmental, Social and Governance) funds such as the JUST Capital ETF (Exchange-Traded Fund) now focus on public companies with high levels of customer, employee and community engagement and sustainable management practices.

As more CEOs get on board and lead a strategic and systematic approach to engaging all stakeholders, those at large organizations will either accept responsibility for the role of Chief Engagement Officer with the support of a single executive or will need to put someone in charge of the effort.

With so much research, empirical evidence and common-sense linking enterprise-wide engagement to financial results, it's clear that every organization can benefit from aligning the interests of all stakeholders in the organization's brand, values, mission, goals and objectives.

The challenge? Most organizations silo engagement between multiple executives so that no one is truly accountable, with the CEO often mediating between competing factions for resources and priorities. The role of the CEO, with or without the support of the Chief Engagement Officer, is to oversee a strategy to ensure the organization delivers its brand promises, not only to consumers but to all sales and non-sales employees, distribution partners, vendors and communities to ensure that everyone has similar expectations and understands how they can benefit from or contribute to the organization.

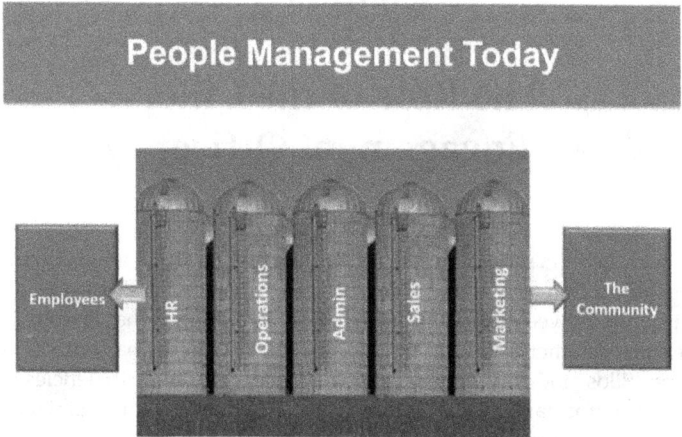

People Management Today

BUST UP THE SILOS

The Chief Engagement Officer must have the authority to bust up the silos and eliminate the politics to keep the entire organization focused on common goals rather than infighting for resources and standing. This means that in the new world of the people-centric CEO, human resources, sales, marketing, customer service, operations and compliance — any group in which people are the primary resource or customer — will either report to the Chief Engagement Officer, or the CEO will designate that this person is the stand-in for the CEO in all Enterprise Engagement-related matters. CEOs at larger companies who decide to assume this role on their own will still need the help of a full-time senior level executive, as the scope of the job, as outlined below, is simply too much for a CEO to implement with so many other responsibilities.

Either way, the CEO must be the unwavering heart and soul of the Enterprise Engagement process, making a point to get face-to-face with all stakeholders in a way that demonstrates genuine interest and an open ear, and that actively and personally supports every key strategic and tactical element of the Enterprise Engagement plan. He or she will build into almost every day's schedule the style advocated by author Tom Peters: MBWA — manage by walking around.

Here's what a CEO-led Enterprise Engagement organization looks like:

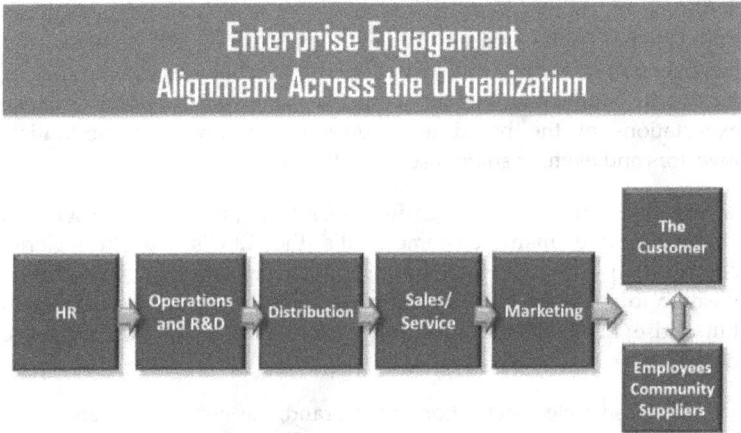

Enterprise Engagement Alignment Across the Organization

ENGAGE ALL STAKEHOLDERS IN A SYSTEMATIC WAY

When ISO (The International Organization for Standardization) determined in the last decade that it had failed to address the issue of people in its quality, safety and 58 other management standards, the Technical Committee didn't just consider employees, but rather *all* stakeholders. The new Annex SL requirements now embedded in 60 ISO standards specifically call for a CEO-led strategic and systematic approach to addressing the needs of all interested parties — employees, customers, distribution partners, vendors, communities, regulators...in other words, anyone who touches the organization.

The challenge is that most organizations aren't set up to look at all stakeholders holistically. Most divide the management of customers, sales and non-sales employees, vendors and communities into multiple fiefdoms, so that departmental leadership often works at cross-purposes, or worse. Great organizations break down these silos to align the interests of all stakeholders toward common goals. Research on successful organizations finds that sustainable performance comes not just from having engaged customers or dedicated employees, but from having all stakeholders engaged in a common definition of the brand and its values, mission, goals and value proposition to its various stakeholders.

The process of managing the needs of all interested parties in a large organization is a full-time job, and not one that involves the traditional definition of Human Resources Manager or what some organizations call Chief People Officer. Why? Because the job involves the management of not just employees but all stakeholders and requires as much an understanding of consumer and distribution partner expectations of the brand as it does of employees, communities, investors and even, in some cases, regulators.

At organizations small enough for CEOs to regularly engage with all employees and many customers, it's the CEO's job. In a large organization—one with perhaps over 100 employees—it's a full-time position to assist the CEO, as can be seen by these core elements of an Enterprise Engagement Operating System (see Chapter 3 for more detail):

1) Establish a clear definition of the brand, mission, values, goals and the role of the CEO in promoting the effort throughout the year.

2) Create and manage an Enterprise Engagement Business Plan or Operating System to direct the organization's activities in a strategic and systematic manner.

3) Make every attempt to ensure that the right leaders and employees are recruited and developed for the right jobs consistent with the brand, values (culture) and objectives.

4) Regularly assess, survey, or obtain feedback from all stakeholders—customers, distribution partners, employees, vendors, communities, etc.—as relevant.

5) Ensure open communication to create a community, inform and reinforce values and connections.

6) To the extent possible, design jobs that not only maximize productivity, but also quality and retention by considering the human need for empowerment, self-determination and flexibility.

7) Ensure that training in the workplace is both strategic (in that it reminds people of their role in the organization) and tactical (in

that it gives them the skills to not only succeed at their jobs but also to fulfill their capabilities and aspirations).

8) Create a sense of community and dynamism by encouraging collaboration at work and support Corporate Social Responsibility efforts and diversity.

9) Establish a process of rewards and recognition that surprises, delights and emotionally moves people who demonstrate through their actions the values of the organization and what's needed to achieve goals.

10) Seriously monitor all the qualitative and quantitative data for ROI, and in large organizations mine it to discover what within your overall culture fosters sustainable dedication.

11) The CEO will be responsible for any disclosures an organization chooses to make to investors and other stakeholders.

Of any position in a major company, the CEO and/or Chief Engagement Officer will have among the most measurable in terms of performance, because the measures will include the very same metrics that many public companies eventually will be compelled to either voluntarily (or in some countries mandatorily) disclose:

- Number of full-time/salaried employees and independent contractors, compared with previous years.

- Overall payroll compared with previous years.

- Overall nonpayroll expenses (incentives, recognition, benefits, training, excluding taxes), and as a percentage of payroll.

- Employee retention (percentage retained year-to-year).

- Number of independent contractors (compared with previous years) and overall expenditures on independent contractors.

- Customer retention (percentage retained year-to-year).

- Overall expenditures in marketing and sales costs, and as a percentage of overall sales, compared with previous years.

- Number of reportable accidents/deaths compared with previous years.

- Expenditures in Corporate Social Responsibility, with comparisons.

- Number of lawsuits (by employee, customer, community), with year-over-year comparison.

- Successful implementation of the current year's overall Enterprise Engagement Operating System or plan.

CHIEF ENGAGEMENT OFFICER QUALIFICATIONS

Because so many executives get siloed into operations, sales, marketing, human resources and finance, one of the big challenges will be finding senior executives who have; a) the executive authority to figuratively "knock heads" in order to break down silos and build alignment; b) the listening and empowerment skills necessary to inspire engagement; and c) the broad set of skills and challenges to weave together a holistic solution. From a skills and experience standpoint, the Chief Engagement Officer should have a fundamental understanding of and experience with:

1) Brand, culture and organizational values and how to build alignment around a common value proposition for all stakeholders.

2) How recruitment and leadership development can support and align with the organizational strategy.

3) The role of assessment, surveys and feedback tools and how to make sure the right information gets to the right people and is acted upon expeditiously.

4) Every form of communication, from digital and print to face-to-face and three-dimensional, to make sure that the overall brand, values and goals are effectively conveyed to all stakeholders.

5) Learning platforms and how they need to be tied to an overall organizational development strategy that supports the brand proposition.

6) Job design strategies that seek to make people more productive, engaged and quality conscious, and which build flexibility into the workplace to promote job-sharing efficiencies.

7) Innovation and collaboration practices that sustain continuous improvement.

8) Community and diversity strategies to create a culture of inclusion and warmth.

9) How to structure rewards and recognition programs to support both extrinsic and intrinsic motivation and communicate organizational values.

10) The role of technology and how it can be used to create a community, enhance information flow and address all levers of engagement in an auditable way.

11) Measurement, analytics and prescriptive use of data.

12) Human Capital disclosure issues and formats.

If your organization seeks to improve efficiencies through an Enterprise Engagement or other Operating System, the Chief Engagement Officer might also serve as the chief implementor of that process.

Sound like a tall order? It is, which is one explanation for why such an obvious and necessary role has taken a generation to emerge.

The Enterprise Engagement Academy at EEA.tmlu.org and *Enterprise Engagement: The Roadmap 5th Edition*, available on Amazon.com and most online bookstores, are specifically designed to provide a more complete desk reference for CEOs or Chief Engagement Officers aspiring to apply a strategic and systematic approach to engaging all stakeholders.

Chapter 6

CEO Profiles

The stories of six CEOs who have earned the
ISO 10018 Honorary CEO Citation for
Quality People Management from the
Enterprise Engagement Alliance

- Kenneth Frazier, CEO, Merck & Co.
- Hubert Joly, CEO Emeritus, Best Buy
- Jim McCann, CEO Emeritus, 1-800-FLOWERS.COM, Inc.
- Bill McDermott, CEO, SAP
- Gay Vaynerchuk, CEO, VaynerMedia
- Colleen Wegman, CEO, Wegman's

Without calling their organizational leadership process by any name,
these six leaders have demonstrated a strategic and sustainable
approach to success through the engagement of all stakeholders.

**Honorary CEO Citation for
Quality People Management**

Kenneth Frazier,
CEO, Merck & Co.

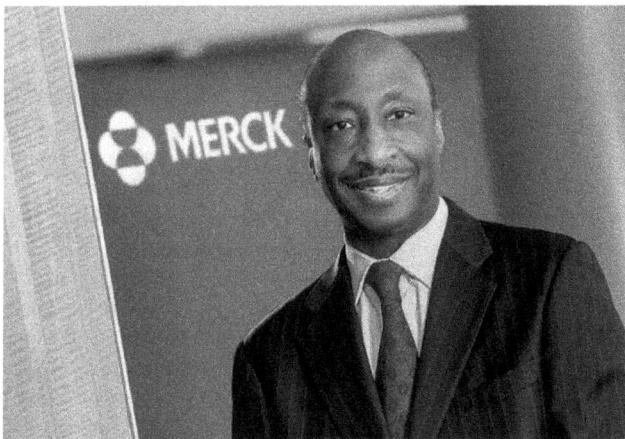

The leadership style of Kenneth C. Frazier, CEO of Merck & Co., stands in stark contrast to that of another of our winners, Gary Vaynerchuk of VaynerMedia, proving that the principles of ISO 10018 standards and Enterprise Engagement leave plenty of room for creative flexibility. While we honored Vaynerchuk in part for his outspoken advocacy for business principles that put people first, we honor Kenneth Frazier for his strategic and systematic but much more low-key approach to engaging all stakeholders that are well documented in the company's 2017-2018 Corporate Responsibility Report. The report provides detailed information of interest to ESG (Environmental, Social and Governance) investors on its strategies, practices and outcomes that provide a model for other organizations of any type seeking to voluntarily disclose their sustainable management practices and outcomes.

Because Frazier has written no books yet, shows little inclination to seek publicity, or work the social media or speaking circuit, the best advice CEOs will get from him are from studying his stunning accomplishments. This profile focuses on a distinguished track record of addressing the interests of all stakeholders in a systematic fashion, with less in the way of personal CEO-to-CEO advice available from other leaders profiled because Frazier is such a low-key leader. That said, this single statement to Black Enterprise magazine perhaps best sum's up Frazier's management philosophy: "There are lots of examples of companies that have lost their way because they've sort of lost their soul, which is a funny word to use, but companies do have souls."

While these profiles are focused on helping CEOs and their teams learn formal practices from other CEOs and don't seek to explain how each of them arrived at similar conclusions about leadership, it is worth noting that Frazier's path to a strategic focus on success through people is surprising on multiple fronts. Apart from the fact that he rose to this lofty position from the humblest of financial circumstances (his mother died when he was only 12 and his father was a janitor who was essentially self-taught but read two newspapers a day), Frazier didn't cut his teeth in sales, marketing, or operations, but rather in the legal department. After graduating from Harvard Law School, he worked for a major law firm that handled the Merck account before eventually joining the pharmaceutical company's legal department. He made a name for himself at Merck by what was viewed by the company as the successful outcome of the Vioxx inflammatory drug litigation. He was named President in 2007 and became CEO in 2011.

Frazier never held an operational position at the company, yet he has presided over a long period of growth, with the company earning high scores in the social and human capital areas of interest to the Enterprise Engagement Alliance, the International Center for Enterprise Engagement and ESG investors. Merck's board of directors decided to amend the company's mandatory retirement age of 65 years to allow him to continue to serve as CEO.

IMPRESSIVE BENEFITS TO STAKEHOLDERS

In addition to the many lives saved or enhanced through Merck's top-selling cancer drug Keytruda, credited with putting President Jimmy

Carter's brain cancer into remission; Januvia for diabetes, the Gardasil vaccine for certain HPV viruses and numerous other pharmaceuticals, Merck has an outstanding record demonstrating a strategic and systematic approach to engaging all stakeholders documented in relative detail in its *Corporate Responsibility Report.*

Over the last five years, Merck & Co. has delivered impressive returns to shareholders in dividends (nearly 3% on average) and growth, outperforming its peer group of stocks by 12% and the S&P 500 by 8% over the last five years based on steady sales increases and by cost reductions due to major staff cuts earlier in Frazier's tenure. With 69,000 employees and $42 billion in sales, the company has a staggering $613,000 in revenue per employee, compared with about $270,000 at technology company SAP, whose CEO Bill McDermott was also a winner of the ISO 10018 Honorary CEO Citation for Quality People Management.

The company has good Glassdoor.com scores of 3.7 out of 5, 72% of reviewers would recommend the company to a friend and 83% approve of CEO Frazier. The company has won recognition from dozens of organizations worldwide for its ESG investments, including, to name just a few:

Fortune. Frazier was named to the No. 5 spot on *Fortune's* World's Greatest 50 Leaders list.

Corporate Knights. Merck ranked No. 13 among *Corporate Knights'* 2018 Global 100 Most Sustainable Corporations in the World.

Fortune. The company ranked No. 4 on its 50 Best Workplaces for Giving Back.

Corporate Responsibility. *Corporate Responsibility magazine* ranked it No. 22 on its 19th annual 100 Best Corporate Citizens list.

Dividend Channel. Merck was named a 2018 Top Socially Responsible Dividend Stock by *Dividend Channel*, signifying a high-performing stock with above-average "Dividend Rank" statistics, including a strong 3% yield, as well as being recognized by prominent asset managers as a socially responsible investment.

Just Capital. Named to the 2018 JUST 100 List of companies that perform best on issues most Americans care about

Merck has been recognized for best practices by Diversity Best Practices, Equal Opportunity magazine, G.I. Jobs magazine, Healthcare Businesswomen's Association, Human Rights Campaign (HRC) Foundation, LATINA Style magazine, National Association for Female Executives; National Business Group on Health, National Organization on Disability, U.S. Veterans magazine; Working Mother magazine, Workplace Gender Equality Agency and many more.

A STRATEGIC AND SYSTEMATIC PLAN

The company's detailed Corporate Responsibility Report goes well beyond any disclosures required of public companies by the Securities & Exchange Commission and provides a benchmark for organizations of any type seeking to share their sustainable management practices with their stakeholders.

Brand, culture and values that embrace all stakeholders. Merck's code of conduct reads: "Our values and standards are the basis of our success. They always have been. They always will be. The people who use, recommend or prescribe our products have placed their trust in us. No matter how strong our reputation, we must re-earn that trust every day by practicing the values and standards that have guided this company for more than 100 years.

"We work hard to make sure that the integrity of this company remains a priority for every one of our employees, every day, at every level of our company. Our code of conduct, which we publish for employees under the title *Our Values and Standards*, helps to make sure that our employees understand what is expected of them, and provides guidance on business standards and practices. This is just one of the many ways that we continually reinforce the values on which this company was built."

The company's mission, the report says, "is to discover and develop important medicines and vaccines that help solve the world's greatest health care challenges…For more than a century, we have considered it our responsibility to create value for our stakeholders while also contributing to societal objectives. Our *2017/2018 Corporate Responsibility Report* reviews our progress in line with our commitment and global goals. It focuses on our four corporate responsibility priority areas: expanding access to our medical breakthroughs, building a robust and resilient workforce, promoting environmental sustainability, and operating on a foundation of ethical, transparent behavior. There is increasing interest and a growing belief that a company's ethical impact can serve as a barometer for its value and long-term sustainability. We welcome this focus."

An enterprise approach. The company's leadership development program focuses specifically on an organization-wide perspective. The report says that the company strives to reach "deeper, wider and earlier in the organization to develop top talent. We are striving to develop a cross-functional general management mind-set, enterprise-wide knowledge of the business and end-to-end thinking for top talent and potential leaders early in their careers."

Employee engagement. The report states: "We strive to foster employee engagement at our company by promoting a positive work environment and by communicating proactively with all employees.

Research shows that engaged employees work more efficiently and effectively, are motivated to perform beyond minimal expectations, and consequently contribute more desirable business outcomes to the organization. Employee engagement is achieved through trust, mutual commitment and transparent communication. As we do with our external stakeholders, we work to understand our employees' concerns, needs and thoughts pertaining to our company's strengths and weaknesses, while at the same time informing them of our business strategy and progress toward our goals."

The company's annual report includes among its risks: "Failure to attract and retain highly qualified personnel could affect the company's ability to successfully develop and commercialize products. The company's success is largely dependent on its continued ability to attract and retain highly qualified scientific, technical and management personnel, as well as personnel with expertise in clinical research and development, governmental regulation and commercialization. Competition for qualified personnel in the pharmaceutical industry is intense."

Assessment and feedback. The company reports that it has had a steady increase in the response to its bi-annual annual employee engagement survey to 85% in 2016 (the last year reported) from 77% in 2013; with a favorable response of 82% versus 78% in 2013, defined as feeling engaged, enabled and energized. The Culture Index, measuring customer focus, reputation and trust, and innovation, scored 72% for 2016, against 70% in 2013.

The company reports that it "enables employees to provide feedback through a community platform on its enterprise communications platform called Sync and via brief, three- to five-question surveys and open-comment forms attached to key communications. Soliciting employee feedback on the subject of the communication in real time gives us the information we need to close knowledge gaps and address employee concerns. Such direct employee feedback has resulted in meet-and-greet sessions, hosted by our CEO and members of our company's executive committee to provide employees with another opportunity to share information with senior leaders in a more personal setting. Real-time employee sentiment is voluntarily submitted during our quarterly employee business briefings through a widget in our webcast application. This sentiment data provides valuable insights into workplace satisfaction, engagement and culture."

Communications. "We conduct global employee briefings every quarter. Our CEO and members of executive committee speak to employees about how we are fulfilling our company mission and goals. These sessions cover topics such as the quarterly financial performance update, pipeline progress, customer stories, anticipated product developments and a question and answer discussion.

Through Sync, "employees worldwide can gain access to company news and videos, divisional and functional news channels, and organizational communities that allow them to share interests, messages and ideas online. Other employee communications vehicles include quarterly Employee Business Briefings, periodic town hall meetings, email communications from senior management, and employee surveys — in particular, the Voice Survey, which is distributed to all employees on a biannual basis."

The company has an "anonymous helpline, which operates in accordance with applicable legal standards for employee-based hotlines, is available 24/7 to listen and provide advice to employees worldwide." An ombudsman is also available to field calls about ethical or other concerns.

Innovation. Frazier made innovation a foundation of his strategy, leading a major investment in research and development and bringing in a R&D chief Roger Perlmutter, under whose tenure the company released the break-through cancer-drug Keytruda. In addition, the company bakes innovation into the culture in multiple ways. "We leverage the business insights of our U.S. employees, including those who are members of DRIVEN (Delivering Real Insights Via Employee

Networks), to support our company's business objectives. DRIVEN represents true innovation in the pharmaceutical industry and allows us to adopt the best practices from other industries to get the quick, cost-effective and deep insights we need to drive our business forward, asking our own employees to share their experiences—as parents, caregivers, patients, and consumers—so we can serve patients better."

DRIVEN enables employees "to make meaningful contributions to the business in a private, online market-research community. Employees have already contributed to helping us innovate in pet tracking and the use of robotic systems (like the Amazon Echo) for taking care of elderly family members' health. DRIVEN has also been used to make patient and caregiver education resources more relevant by giving feedback on online materials and advertisements. This enables the efficient and compliant engagement of employees to provide business, customer, brand and research development insights via market research methods. We have grown the DRIVEN community to 2,000 employees and had significant cost savings by harnessing the experience of our own employees. It has enabled us to innovate with the patient perspective included for understanding in therapeutic areas like chronic cough, Alzheimer's and the use of new technologies to help with compliance/adherence."

Wellness. The Corporate Responsibility section on employees includes detailed information on the company's wellness program and efforts to address emotional, social and financial well-being of interest to CEOs and their teams seeking to benchmark or develop their own practices. Merck's *LIVE IT* well-being platform includes four pillars: PREVENT IT, BALANCE IT, MOVE IT and FUEL IT. The company promotes "offerings within each of these areas to engage and enhance the lives of our employees." LIVE IT reportedly was launched in the United States in 2011 and now is available in over 40 countries, reaching approximately 78% of the company's global workforce, the company reports.

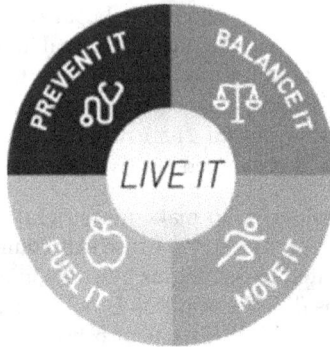

Safety. The report provides extensive details relative to that disclosed by most companies on safety. "We have worked steadily over the last five years to drive down our workplace injury rates. In 2017, our lost-time injury rate remained at 0.13, the same as 2016. Our recordable injury rate was 0.33, down 6% from the prior year. Last year, 29% of our recordable injuries were related to slips, trips and falls, with motor vehicle and 'struck-by/caught-in' injuries accounting for 24% and 21% of the total number of injuries, respectively. We saw a 31% decrease in the number of ergonomic recordable injuries in 2017 versus the prior year. Consistency in our case management process as well as improvements to our facilities and related equipment contributed to the decrease in these types of injuries," the company reported.

"In 2017, we continued to see reductions in the number of motor vehicle-related injuries, with an 11% improvement versus the prior year. Our global vehicle safety program includes a standard duty of care by holding both employees and managers accountable for achieving safe driving expectations.

We also continue to focus our efforts on slip, trip and fall injuries. In addition to our focus on facility maintenance, we coach colleagues to understand their surroundings, take necessary precautions, and make better decisions to avoid these types of injuries."

Diversity. The company reports that 49% of new hires in 2017 were women; 40% of management roles were held by women; 36% of U.S. employees recruited were from under-represented ethnic groups, and 23% of U.S. executives are from under-represented ethnic groups.

Frazier's commitment to diversity goes back to the year he took over as CEO. "As a leader in global healthcare, we are committed to addressing critical social, environmental and economic challenges to ensure not only the vitality of our business, but also the health of our world," he says in Merck's *2011 Corporate Responsibility Report.* Frazier reportedly ties his executive compensation to diversity metrics, personally signs off on diversity goals and meets with resource groups regularly. In 2011, he signed the CEO statement of support for the Women's Empowerment Principles, a project of the United Nations Development Fund for Women and the United Nations Global Compact. He is Merck's first African-American CEO and one of six Black CEOs at Fortune 500 companies.

Learning and development. The latest *Corporate Responsibility Report* offers extensive information on the company's professional development strategies. "The Global Learning & Development organization, under the leadership of the chief learning officer, deploys a global approach to maximizing the value of learning and development investments by leveraging resources, educational platforms and other synergies across the enterprise to deliver learning solutions designed to optimize business and customer outcomes. To support our global employee base, we sponsor curricula that build leadership and management skills as well as provide technical and functional training to all employees. We have five active Key Talent Programs to support the learning and development of our future key talent, women in leadership, diverse talent, and those who are at the executive level. These programs support the advancement of our talent pipeline and diversity and inclusion strategy." The programs include:

- **General Management Acceleration Program (GMAP)** — the company's flagship program to develop future global, enterprise-wide leaders. "The Office of the CEO sponsors the program. Successful participants will broaden their experience and perspective, enhance their leadership abilities and be well-placed to grow into positions of greater responsibility following their rotations. The objective of GMAP is to create a robust global acceleration program for internal talent, providing the right experiences and learning opportunities to grow broad, global business leaders to meet our future business demand."

- **The Business Leadership Program** — a global program to "enhance both an individual's leadership and business acumen skills. Areas of focus include: our company's strategic context and how to integrate long-term plans with short-term action; value creation in financial and non-financial terms so one is able to increase his/her ability to perform in the short-term and plan for the long-term; and ability to translate strategy into action to deliver business impact."

- **The Women's Leadership Program** — the company's global program to support the advancement of women into senior leadership ranks. "Areas of focus include: strengthening the ability to navigate within the organization; gaining skills and knowledge to grow and improve leadership capacity; and increasing the ability to manage gender differences and any subtle 'micro-inequities' that may exist in the culture."

- **Diverse Leader Program** — this U.S.-only program "is an interactive leadership journey that is designed to create a safe place where participants can hone their leadership skills while exploring what it means to be a leader of color within the company. While building leadership proficiency, participants will also investigate the similarities and differences of leaders from other racial/ethnic groups. Finally, they will have the opportunity to deepen relationships with their sponsors/mentors through experiential activities and guided and unguided conversations."

- **Leadership Development Center** — the Leadership Development Center is a website that features videos, articles, program announcements and resources for leaders and managers. Resources are aligned to our leadership behaviors, professional competencies, and functional competencies, and are available in the following formats: "on-demand" Web-based modules, classroom programs, articles, books (including audio books), webcasts and suggestions for "on-the-job" development activities.

- **Team development** — "For teams, there is a suite of programs that provide skills and tools for team leaders and team members, including Leading High Performing Teams, Virtual Teaming, Assessing Team Performance, Teaming Fundamentals, and Insights Discovery, a program to understand communications styles."

The company reports that employees completed a total of 5.3 million training courses in 2017, versus 4.2 million in 2016; 2.6 million total hours of training in 2017 versus 2.1 million hours the prior year; and that each employee completed 48 courses in 2017 versus 69 the year before. The number of leaders participating in training in 2017 was nearly double the number in 2015, it said.

Career laddering. The company's myCareer, platform "serves as our global gateway to professional development, performance management, talent management and learning across the company. It keeps track of employee development plans, performance objectives and performance ratings, career aspirations (desired next roles and mobility preferences), experience (both outside of and within the company), language proficiency, certifications and education. The primary business purpose of myCareer is to facilitate more effective, consistent and efficient companywide performance management, talent reviews, succession planning, and associated employee performance and development processes through a single, integrated and automated global system of record for critical talent data about our employees. This helps to ensure that our workforce continues to realign itself with company objectives."

Total rewards. The company discloses extensive information on its "total rewards package." The report states: "One way in which we recognize their importance is to provide a valuable suite of compensation and benefit programs as well as resources to support our employees' professional achievement and personal well-being. Together, we call these 'Total Rewards.' Total Rewards include compensation and financial rewards, health and insurance benefits, opportunities for employees to develop their skills and grow their careers, and programs that help meet the demands of managing employees' professional and personal well-being. Our philosophy behind these programs is rooted in maintaining our competitive position in the market while providing a comprehensive and valuable package of rewards to attract and retain a talented and diverse workforce."

The company's "myTotalRewards online personalized resource provides U.S. employees with a simple, consolidated view of their total compensation and financial rewards at our company." For most active employees (certain groups are excluded, such as those that are subject to collective bargaining), my Total Rewards contains the following detailed information:

Money: Annual pay, cash incentives and the company's estimated contribution to pension, 401(k), insurance, and other benefits.
Health: The value of the key health benefits in which an employee participates, including medical, dental and vision coverage.
Retirement & Long-Term Incentives: Retirement benefits and long-term incentives—and how they've performed over time.

Other Rewards: Other benefits available, such as educational assistance, K–12 educational guidance and financial planning.

For employees who are subject to collective bargaining obligations within and outside of the U.S., the company says that it complies "with any and all applicable contractual and legal obligations in providing information to employees." Merck claims that "it's health and well-being, retirement and insurance programs draw from best practices to ensure quality, competitive value, protection from significant financial hardship and access to tools and resources to support employees and their family members at all life stages."

Community. As one can imagine, Merck has an extensive Corporate Social Responsibility plan that includes drug donation programs, patient assistance with medicine costs, and patient assistance programs for drug purchases. According to an interview in Life Science Leader with Brenda Colatrella, Executive Director of Merck's Office of Corporate Responsibility and President of the Merck Foundation, the company defines "corporate [social] responsibility as a commitment to developing creative and innovative solutions to global health challenges while at the same time building our business in a sustainable way. While philanthropy is an important demonstration of our commitment to being a responsible corporate citizen, our commitment to corporate responsibility actually goes beyond that and is reflected in our business practices as well. About every five years we conduct a corporate responsibility materiality assessment to determine if we are focusing on the issues that matter most to our stakeholders from a CR perspective. From the most recent assessment, we affirmed our four CR priority areas for Merck: (1) Access to healthcare; (2) Environmental sustainability; (3) Employee health and wellbeing; and (4) Ethics and transparency."

Supplier engagement. As part of its enterprise engagement approach to management, the report details requirements and expectations related to its relationships with all vendors, including systems, performance, labeling, packaging, and shipping, and other practices.

ADVICE FROM FRAZIER

Although a member of the American Philosophical Society, Frazier does not actively dole out his views, frequently give advice in media interviews, or appear to actively promote his perspectives in public speaking. Here are a few of the insights he has shared over the years.

Stick to your principles. Despite the influence of many mentors, and professors at Harvard, etc. he stresses the advice he got from his father to not worry about what others think. As reported in FiercePharma.com, "After becoming CEO, Frazier stopped providing long-term earnings guidance to Wall Street analysts, and he resisted the 'immense' pressure Big Pharma CEOs were facing at the time to cut research and development spending while at the same time cutting about 12,000 jobs to lower the company's fixed costs after its merger with Schering Plough."

He told the writer: "I knew what this company was about was the science," Frazier said. "I just had to tune out all the critics." Ultimately, he added, those critics applauded the decision.

Lead, don't follow. "Don't bow to any pressure to blindly follow industry trends or to shy away from controversial strategies. Just avoiding risk doesn't make a company successful."

Be willing to take a moral stance. As a young man after law school, Frazier spent time in Soweto, South Africa to provide legal assistance. In his early days working as a lawyer before joining Merck, he defended a man on death row who was eventually released. His leadership in the aggressive case-by-case defense of the company in the Vioxx litigation was rooted, he said, in his conviction that the company acted in good faith. Many believe his legal strategy significantly reduced the company's overall financial exposure.

Beware of hierarchy. "One of the challenges associated with a company becoming large is that companies become hierarchical. They become bureaucratic. They become slow. They become risk averse."

Have personal performance measures. "Because of the importance of what we do at Merck as a company, I have two metrics by which to measure success during my time leading Merck: 1. How many people do we help? 2. How much help did we give them? I want to be able to say that I was a good steward of an organization that serves as a tremendous force for good."

Note: While generally a low-key CEO, Frazier drew widespread attention when he was among a group of CEOs who resigned their memberships in the American Manufacturing Council early in the Trump administration after taking issue with the president's characterization of the demonstrators at the rally in Charlottesville, VA. This decision did not factor in any way in our selection of Frazier for this honorary citation. The concept of Enterprise

Engagement is strictly non-partisan, and a CEO's politics has nothing to do with his or her selection for this designation.

**Honorary CEO Citation for
Quality People Management**

Hubert Joly, CEO Emeritus, Best Buy

It's no surprise that Hubert Joly staked his successful turnaround strategy at Best Buy on a strategic focus on people. After all, he joined Best Buy after an eight-year stint as President of Carlson Wagonlit (and later its parent, Carlson Companies), which was founded by Curt Carlson, one of the inventors of the modern loyalty and incentive fields. When Joly joined Best Buy in 2012, the company was a brand tarnished by high-pressure sales tactics, high employee turnover and poor service, in danger of extinction as a result of competition from Amazon. He has since led an extraordinary success story. The company's stock has risen from the $20 range five years ago to averaging over $60 a share today, and annual earnings per share have more than doubled over the last four years.

THE STATS DON'T LIE

Joly has proven that a turnaround artist doesn't necessarily have to be a cold-hearted villain. Of more than 18,000 ratings on Glassdoor.com, 92% approve of the Best Buy CEO, versus 85% for Amazon's Jeff Bezos, and the company's Glassdoor rating of 3.8 (out of 5) is very good for the retail business. The company's employee turnover rate is down to 30% from 60%, according to the *Minneapolis Tribune*, and Best Buy's American Customer Satisfaction Index score of 77% is not far below the highest reported rating (82%) on the organization's scale. Joly told the *Tribune* that the true measure of success is "brand love," measured by revenue per customer. He believes this is achieved by "human magic," or creating a deep relationship with people that creates a flywheel effect that in turn creates more stability. On his Wikipedia page, Joly writes: "We believe that price-competitiveness is table stakes. The way we want to win is around the advice, convenience, service."

A *Fortune* magazine article reported: "And while Joly has now earned a reputation as a respected turnaround artist, investors say he does not fit the negative stereotype of other such executives." The article quoted analyst Joe Feldman Senior Managing Director of Telsey Group, a consumer research advisory group, as saying Joly is "...more of a leader than just one of those guys that comes in and cuts the crap out of everything and leaves."

MOVING CAUTIOUSLY

When Joly took over the struggling Best Buy in 2012, one of the first things he did was get behind the counter at a retail store in the guise of an employee, moving cautiously before defining a clear vision. At the time he told Reuters that he "plans to cut non-salary expenses and woo holiday shoppers with a three-pronged strategy of offering competitive prices, stocking the right amount of hot products and improving customer service. Joly declined to be more specific."

Going forward, Joly explained, the plan was "to take advantage of Best Buy's clout with key suppliers by reaching out to them to develop deeper strategic partnerships. There are different ways to skin a cat in terms of a partnership. It can be exclusive [products], it can be unique shopping experiences, it can be deals...you know, a whole variety of things."

Out of this discovery process came the company's turnaround strategy, known as the Renew Blue plan, now in its fifth year. Joly told Retail Intelligence Systems that the success of the effort "is the direct result of the execution of our Renew Blue strategy and the hard work, dedication, and customer focus on the part of all of our associates." The company now has a new CEO, 43-year old Corey Barry, a woman, who was most recently Chief Financial and Strategic Transformation Officer.

A CEO-LED ENTERPRISE ENGAGEMENT STRATEGY

Without calling his strategic process by any specific name, Joly's letter to investors in the company's 2018 annual report provides the classic definition of and framework for an enterprise approach to engagement and a template for other CEOs, whether they run public, private, or not-for-profit or governmental organizations. Below are excerpts from the annual report, demonstrating the company's focus on addressing the key brand definition, vision and goals of a strategic and systematic approach to everyone in the enterprise in order to achieve organizational goals.

"Our performance is highly dependent on attracting, retaining and engaging appropriately qualified employees in our stores, service centers, distribution centers, field and corporate offices. Our strategy of offering high quality services and assistance for our customers requires a highly trained and engaged workforce. The turnover rate in the retail sector is relatively high, and there is an ongoing need to recruit and train new employees. Factors that affect our ability to maintain sufficient numbers of qualified employees include employee morale, our reputation, unemployment rates, competition from other employers, availability of qualified personnel and our ability to offer appropriate compensation packages."

"If we fail to attract, retain and engage appropriately qualified employees, including employees in key positions, our operations and profitability may be harmed."

A CLEAR BRAND VISION

Joly clearly articulates the company's brand vision, strategy, goals and focus in his investor letter.

- "Fiscal 2018 was another milestone year for Best Buy. We declared our Renew Blue transformation over and launched our growth strategy, Best Buy 2020: Building the New Blue. As I will detail in this letter, we have articulated a clear purpose, strategy and set of goals and investments in support of that strategy." (*Note: having an articulated strategic plan is the foundation of an ISO-compliant Enterprise Engagement process -Ed.*)

- "In September 2017, we held an Investor Day and laid out what we believe is a clear and exciting purpose: to enrich our customers' lives through technology. We aim to do this by addressing key human needs in areas including entertainment, productivity, communication, food, security and health and wellness."

- "We have anchored our strategy around a clear purpose of enriching customers' lives through technology. We also have a clear set of values, as reflected in our Code of Business Ethics. We think that having our employees focused on our purpose and a clear set of values is a key driver of both performance and sustainability."

- Joly's letter explains how Best Buy intends to expand its sales of new technology solutions, total tech support and invest in its online experience, associate proficiency and Mobile 2020, a new service to make it easier for customers to select the right plan and set up their phones.

Without revealing specific information that Best Buy's competitors would like to know, Joly articulates brand vision, values, objective, the people and the general tactics the company will employ to achieve its specific goals.

A FOCUS ON ALL STAKEHOLDERS

In the annual report, Joly clearly explains how the company's goals and objectives will address the needs of all stakeholders, another foundational element of Enterprise Engagement:

Customers. "To enable our Best Buy 2020 strategy, we are investing in capabilities and tools. For example, we are making technology investments in enterprise customer relationship management and knowledge management tools, which will help us build a more seamless and effective experience for our customers and pave the way towards a more relationship-based approach to the customer experience we offer. We are also building out a new services platform to help power our Total Tech Support offering and provide the ability for customers to get easy and quick access to our Geek Squad tech experts, including a new app with video chat capability."

Employees. Joly's investor letter devotes considerable attention to employees:

- "We are investing in our people through recruiting, training, development and compensation. We will continue to invest in specialty labor in areas such as appliances, In-Home Advisor and smart home. We are also investing in the multi-year strategic transformation of our supply chain that is designed to expand our bandwidth for growth and speed."

- "In the context of our improved performance and the expected savings brought about by tax reform, we are increasing the level of investment in the enablers necessary to propel our strategy. Specifically, this includes investments in specialty labor, improvements to employee benefit programs, and an increase in our fiscal 2019 capital expenditure plans to $850 to $900 million from the expectations we shared at Investor Day of $750 to $850 million. This compares to an average capital expenditure of $640 million over the last three fiscal years." The company reportedly used the proceeds of its 2017 tax reform benefits to invest in benefits for employees, including a child-care backup service.

- "We are proud of the environment in which our employees operate, and of the strong levels of employee engagement and satisfaction we are achieving. We invest in the long-term development, effectiveness and engagement of our employees by working to ensure that we have a diverse workforce and inclusive environment, robust training and development programs, and a culture where our people can thrive. We received a perfect score of 100 in the Human Rights Campaign Foundation's Corporate Equality Index and are ranked tenth in the world for employee training and development by *Training* magazine."

- "At the end of fiscal 2018, we employed approximately 125,000 full-time, part-time, and seasonal employees in the U.S., Canada, Mexico, and our sourcing office in China. We consider our employee relations to be good. We offer our employees a wide array of company-paid benefits that vary within our company due to customary local practices and statutory requirements, which we believe are competitive locally and in the aggregate relative to others in our industry."

- "We operate in a competitive labor market and there is a risk that market increases in compensation could have a material adverse effect on our profitability. Failure to recruit or retain qualified employees in the future may impair our efficiency and effectiveness and our ability to pursue growth opportunities. In addition, a significant amount of turnover of our executive team or other employees in key positions with specific knowledge relating to us, our operations, and our industry may negatively impact our operations."

Vendors. "We partner with our vendors to help commercialize their innovations and bring them to life for the consumer. The company accomplishes this through customer-focused curation of the technology it sells online and in stores; effective, targeted marketing that reaches millions of relevant consumers; in-store demonstrations offering hands-on experiences for customers, needs-based selling expertise designed to solve problems and address lifestyle needs; and services that support customers in installing, setting up and operating their technology."

Supply Chain. "We partner with our exclusive brand suppliers to ensure they meet our expectations for safe workplaces where workers are treated fairly. We perform audits, led by either us directly or third parties, to identify any gaps in factory performance and the industry standard code of conduct established by the Responsible Business Alliance. We also provide supplier training and assist in program development to support best practices in relation to conflict minerals, customs and trade antiterrorism measures, and factory labor conditions."

Environment. "We are committed to managing our impact on the environment and are proud of our efforts to lower our carbon footprint, reducing it by 60% by 2020. We operate the most comprehensive e-waste recycling service in the U.S. and have collected more than 1.5 billion pounds of e-waste for recycling since 2009. We are also committed to providing an assortment of sustainable technology, including ENERGY STAR® certified products, and have helped customers realize $707 million in utility savings since 2009."

Community. "Corporate Social Responsibility & Sustainability. We believe businesses exist not only to deliver value to shareholders, but also to positively impact our various stakeholders, including society, and contribute to the common good. This holistic focus is a key responsibility our management and Board take seriously...We are particularly excited about the commitment we have made to help prepare 1 million underserved teens for tech-reliant jobs each year by 2020. This will be accomplished through the operation of our Best Buy Teen Tech Centers (year-round after-school programs), which we plan to expand from 15 today to 60 by 2020; career mentoring and internship opportunities through our Career Pathways Program; hosted Geek Squad Academy events (free, interactive technology camps) across the country; more than 100,000 employee volunteer hours each year; and partnerships with other organizations."

Return on investment. In fiscal 2018, Joly reports that the company achieved $285 million in annualized cost reductions and gross profit optimization for a total of $1.6 billion since it began the Renew Blue program five years ago.

THE SECRET TO A SUCCESFUL TURNAROUND

While Joly is considered a successful turnaround artist, he doesn't fit the negative mold of other such executives, says an article in *Fortune*. Here is Joly's approach to a human-focused turnaround:

- **The Bicycle Theory for Turnarounds.** For the first 18 months, don't even worry about the company's strategy, he says, referencing former IBM CEO Louis Gerstner's 1993 quote, "The last thing IBM needs right now is a vision." Instead, says Joly, ask employees to start pedaling — in other words, challenge them to show what they are capable of, and to do what they can to take the company forward.

- **Cut jobs as a "last resort."** Joly says there are four "levers" to improve profits — and job cuts are the last. The focus must be on increasing revenue and cutting non-salary expenses, including overhead and transportation. Eliminate luxury perks, look for health insurance plan savings, only remove people if all else fails and never announce cuts as if "it's something to brag about."

- **Quantity over quality.** "The difference between great leaders and good leaders is not the quality of their decisions, it's the quantity of their decisions," says Joly. Employees should be empowered to make decisions by tolerating more errors and encouraged to follow their instincts by backing them up when they make a mistake. The idea is to make more decisions and then make smart decisions to correct mistakes.

- **Replace "or" with "and."** When executives pondered whether the priority was to cut costs or increase revenue, Joly's answer was to do both. When executives asked if the goal was to make company's retail employee's happier or to focus on customers, the answer was both. By asking employees to go after two goals, he argues, they can do more in less time and eliminate unnecessary "or" and "and" debates.

- **Whistle while you work.** Joly says people need to have a spring in their step, they need to be full of energy and lift and to believe. "When Best Buy was faced with negative press and predictions that it might go out of business, its demoralized staff looked to Joly and his top executives for motivation and reassurance that their hard work would pay off, and employee morale eventually improved."

- **Track your say-do ratio.** Accountability is key. When people come up with ideas and promises to implement them, follow-through is key.

- **Spread bad news faster than good news.** Joly says he doesn't mind being awakened at night with bad news because "Bad news has to travel at least as fast as good news. We never shoot the messenger from that standpoint, because everyone can mobilize around this."

JOLY'S ADVICE FOR OTHER CEOs AND ASPIRING LEADERS

Here are some excerpts from a *Business Insider* interview with Joly about leadership:

- **Be a purposeful leader.** "Be clear about your purpose in life, what drives you, and make sure it's connected with the purpose of the company. If you're driven by making money or career advancement, that's fine for some roles. But many people want a deeper purpose in their career. You need to make sure that your purpose lines up with that of where you work. Most of us want to do something meaningful. We want to live a purposeful life."

- **Be clear about your role as a leader.** "Do you believe your role as leaders is to be the smartest person in the room, and make sure everybody knows that? Or is it to create an environment in which others can be successful and, you know, blossom and flourish and so forth? Most companies need a leader who is willing to help others succeed, even if it doesn't immediately benefit the leader."

- **Be clear about who you're serving.** "A good leader is focused on serving the customers, not the boss. If you believe you're serving the servants, meaning people on the front line, and your role is to help them be successful, then you've got it."

- **Be a values-driven leader.** "Integrity is really important," Joly says, although he admits that some of his criteria can sound like "propaganda." However, he says that the proof is in the results. Due to an emphasis on ethical, values-driven leadership, Joly claims turnover at Best Buy has significantly decreased over the last five years. "These numbers with turnover and employee satisfaction, really, would not happen if we're just going to tell people, 'Be happy.'"

- **Be an authentic leader.** Joly's final leadership criteria is being yourself. "Work-life balance almost has the connotation that your work is not part of your life. So you can be an a--, the most terrible person at work, and then you can be the most wonderful person outside—it makes no sense." Instead, he urges people to be their full, authentic selves always.

EQ VS. IQ

On a personal note, in an interview with *Retail Wire*, Joly admits that an executive coach helped him realize that one of his biggest quirks was a tendency to think he was "the smartest person in the room." He determined that this trait held back others from contributing. Says Joly: "As I age, I believe that IQ is way over-rated and that EQ is where it matters. It's how you assemble a team and what kind of types of leaders you put in power."

**Honorary CEO Citation for
Quality People Management**

Jim McCann,
CEO Emeritus,
1-800-FLOWERS.COM, Inc.

If anybody understands the role of customers, employees, distribution partners, vendors, and communities in achieving success, it's entrepreneur Jim McCann. He transformed a single flower shop into the $1 billion 1-800-FLOWERS.COM, Inc. business, which now includes (among others) the Harry & David and Cheryl's Cookies brands to provide a complete gifting experience. McCann recently shared what he has learned about the role of Human Capital from his experience turning a humble flower shop business into a household name.

First, for a bit of perspective: Flowers smell and look pretty and bring smiles, delight and comfort, but it's a tough, low-margin business. Probably few places is it tougher than in the streets of New York, where through serendipity Jim McCann as a young man purchased a florist shop, and then purchased a few more to create a franchise business that has reached over $1 billion in sales since going public in 1999. Consumers send flowers for emotional reasons, so the expectation for customer experience is high, but the economics and management issues are anything but trivial because of the low margins and relentless pressure to hold down costs to turn a profit.

THE SIDE OF FLOWERS MOST PEOPLE DON'T SEE

Flowers are perishable and the business is largely seasonal. The business challenges are never-ending given the complexities of the industry, including working with floral shops in which local owners have significant control over the culture they create in their stores. As such, the company moved to diversify its offerings. Today, its Gourmet Food and Gift Baskets segment represents more than half of the company's overall revenue. Over the last five years, the company's financial performance has continued to accelerate, and its stock price has more than tripled.

1-800-FLOWERS.COM, Inc. is quite clear about its culture and principles. Its pledge to customers: "We're obsessed with providing a terrific experience. If not, we'll make it right—guaranteed." The company makes a clear effort to help prepare employees and vendors leading up to and during peak periods when people are working overtime through various types of events, and there are regular company-wide update meetings with current CEO Chris McCann. Walk around the organization's headquarters in Carle Place, NY, and one can't help but see placards displaying the organization's values:

Be Constructive. Make and solicit positive, constructive suggestions every day.
Be Positive. Teach others to have fun and celebrate success each day. Use positive language and reduce negative language.
Be Prompt. Do it now...Answer it now...Fix it now!
Be Outcome Focused. Find positive lessons in every adverse situation. Use the past only for positive lessons.
Be Reflective. Look for important positive lessons. What could you have done to make something better?
Be Relentless. Seek positive incremental improvement every day.

AN ENTREPRENEUR'S REFLECTION ON PEOPLE

In this Q&A, Jim McCann shares what he has learned about the need to have a strategic and systematic approach to stakeholder engagement.

What made you conclude that engaging all your stakeholders — customers, employees, vendors, communities — was a strategic rather than tactical initiative?

McCann: At 1-800-FLOWERS.COM, Inc., our mission is "To Deliver Smiles," so it's essential that we have a team that takes pride in the special role they play in helping us accomplish this. From our employees to the vendors we work and partner with, delivering smiles is truly a team effort and one that requires a highly engaged and passionate network of people. Our commitment to having a dedicated and caring team obsessed with service is something that is deeply valued by all our shareholders.

As far as our employees across the enterprise, it's important for them to understand how they contribute to that mission and feel empowered to share fresh ideas — whether it relates to product innovation, new ways to enhance the customer experience, or how to leverage emerging technologies across various facets of the business. We can all learn from one another daily, as everyone brings unique experiences and perspectives to the table. We're a company rooted in entrepreneurism and self-reinvention, so we strive to ensure that every one of our stakeholders understands the strategic direction of the company.

Continuing to enhance the customer experience is at the core of our business, and most of the experimentation and innovation we've done across the company has been to that end. We strive to make it easy for customers to express, connect and celebrate with the important people in their lives. That's why we've transformed into a one-stop gifting destination, featuring an all-star portfolio of about a dozen brands, which now includes Harry & David, Cheryl's Cookies, Simply Chocolate, Wolferman's and The Popcorn Factory, among others.

As a large company that works within local markets nationwide, we're also dedicated to giving back to the communities we serve. We engage in a variety of philanthropic programs aimed at strengthening communities where our employees live and work. Our company's signature philanthropic partner is Smile Farms, a non-profit organization that provides meaningful jobs in agricultural settings to young adults and adults with developmental disabilities, allowing them to master new skills, experience teamwork, contribute to their community and, importantly, take home a paycheck. While it wasn't our end-game, our philanthropic efforts have helped us attract and retain compassionate employees who are deeply-engaged in what we stand for as a company.

What are the key principles of your successful engagement of all stakeholders?

McCann: Our philosophy is to develop relationships first, do business second. This was the exact atmosphere I strived to maintain at my first flower shop in Manhattan in 1976, and it's still a fundamental component of how we position our company culture and engage our stakeholders. When it comes to our employees, we focus on providing fun and educational initiatives that empower them to learn, build meaningful relationships across the business and go the extra mile to deliver smiles. I also host "'What's Up?' Dinners," where I gather rotating groups of employees across all levels and functions to sit down, eat and "ideate" with me in an informal setting. This helps me get to know everyone on a personal level and allows them to develop relationships and become more engaged with the company.

Our 1-800-Flowers.com brand works with thousands of local florists across the nation to deliver smiles, and they play an important role in helping our customers express, connect and celebrate with the most important people in their lives. We value our relationship with these florists, which is why we offer the most innovative technology products, services and educational resources to help them grow through our BloomNet business. Each year, 1-800-Flowers.com hosts Local Artisan Design Workshops, bringing together a select group of talented florists to brainstorm, share ideas and create unique product concepts. The workshop gives our teams the opportunity to work closely with these florists and tap into local trends that resonate well in their markets but can be adapted to share with a nationwide audience through our Local Artisan Collection.

1-800-Flowers.com sources its flowers from premier farms in the U.S. and abroad that follow socially and environmentally responsible practices as certified by industry-leading organizations, such as the Rainforest Alliance, Florverde, Veriflora, Asocolflores, GLOBALG.A.P. and Fair Trade. Our team visits our partner farms multiple times a year to verify they are following best practices and promoting fair and safe working conditions. We understand the important role we play in contributing to a sustainable future.

I've long believed in "doing good while doing business," which is why we began our "Summer of a Million Smiles" (SOMS) program to encourage employee volunteerism and community involvement during the summer season. This annual enterprise-wide tradition encourages employees to identify and support local causes, groups and organizations while spreading countless smiles along the way. SOMS events have included volunteering at soup kitchens and local animal shelters, teaching children with autism how to surf, participating in wheelchair basketball games, hosting fun decorating sessions for local youth groups, building greenhouses to help employees of Smile Farms and so much more. This program really resonates with our employees, and it's something they look forward to each year.

What advice would you have for other CEOs?

McCann: My biggest advice to other CEOs is to not be afraid to "fire" themselves. What I mean by this is for them to trust that they've placed the right people in the right roles, take a step back, and let those individuals do exactly what they were hired to do. This approach enables CEOs to focus holistically on the company, identify the true needs of their stakeholders and continue to develop an overarching culture and broader direction that everyone throughout the organization understands and supports. I'd also advise them to be bold in taking risks and not shy away from the prospect of making a mistake. Since establishing 1-800-FLOWERS.COM, Inc., some of my greatest successes today stem from some of my biggest mistakes of yesterday — and I wouldn't have it any other way.

Tell us how you made the transition when passing the CEO torch to your brother, Chris McCann? What are you doing now?

McCann: After operating as the CEO for more than 40 years and transforming the company from a single floral shop into a true one-stop gifting destination featuring multiple brands, it felt like the right time for me to pass the torch to my brother, Chris. The succession plan through which he became CEO was actually established many years ago, as we wanted to ensure the transition was as smooth as possible.

Chris was already overseeing our company's day-to-day operations, having served as President since 2000. In that role, he helped 1-800-FLOWERS.COM, Inc. surpass $1 billion in revenues while enhancing our market share and industry-leading position, which indicated to me that he was absolutely the right man for the job. Since becoming CEO, Chris has aggressively fostered innovation and has spearheaded the continued growth of the company. I'm extremely proud of what he's accomplished in the role, and I look forward to seeing him continue to transform our company.

Since transitioning from my role as CEO, I remain highly involved in the company as Founder and Chairman, but I've also had more time to manifest my continued desire to create. I established Clarim Holdings a year or so ago. It's a private holding company that expands market opportunities for clients by providing capital along with an extensive network of high-tier support partners. Knowing firsthand how challenging it can be to manage a high-growth company, I structured this network to provide services essential to privately held, founder and family-led companies through a targeted set of verticals. To date, the Clarim at Clarimholdings.com portfolio includes Ascent, Copperfield, The Second Shift, Techonomy and Worth Media, which provide leadership development, advisory and marketing, networking, and media services.

Honorary CEO Citation for
Quality People Management

Bill McDermott, CEO, SAP

How a young man from a middle-class household in Flushing, NY bought a delicatessen at age 16 that would help put him through college and go on to achieve extraordinary success is a story best told in Bill McDermott's book, *Winners Dream, A Journey From Corner Store to Corner Office.* The Enterprise Engagement Alliance honors McDermott for his extraordinary exemplification of 21st-century leadership: a strategic and systematic approach to the management of human capital as an asset, and for fostering the engagement of all stakeholders – customers, employees, distribution partners, vendors, communities, and investors.

SAP's 2018 voluntary annual Integrated Report, what we call a Sustainability Report, most recently published in February 2019, represents a paradigm for 21st-century CEOs seeking to emulate his company's strategic and systematic approach to engaging all stakeholders in its brand, culture, mission and goals. Moreover, the format and content in SAP's Integrated Report provides a benchmark against which other public, private and even not-for-profit organizations can plan, measure and disclose their own efforts to manage what is now finally recognized as an asset: human capital, comprised not just of employees, but customers, distribution partners, vendors and communities.

As a leading supplier of software in customer experience and employee engagement, SAP should be held to a high standard, but with about 96,500 employees worldwide, the ability to strategically and systematically manage human capital with such consistent results and positive outcomes is no small accomplishment.

NOT JUST A POPULARITY CONTEST

McDermott could be selected for the Honorary CEO Citation for Quality People Management designation based just on the company's Glassdoor.com scores alone. Nearly 5,500 employees who have posted on Glassdoor.com give him a 98% positive rating, and 93% of people would recommend the company to a friend. As a technology company, SAP has a major advantage over companies in other industries in that the pay is high, growth opportunities abound, and the working conditions are much above average. That said, the company's Integrated Report demonstrates these sterling stats are no accident, but rather the result of the CEO's strategic and systematic approach to engaging all stakeholders.

While his sparse Wikipedia page contains little in the way of self-promotion, McDermott posts pithy, personal reflections and advice on his LinkedIn page, coming from someone who not only achieved success on his own merits to become the first American CEO of a European technology company, but who also bounced back rapidly after the loss of an eye in a 2015 accident. His LinkedIn profile and writings suggest a hard-working, focused executive; yet he apparently has a light-hearted side and, having come up through the ranks from sales, is known to enthusiastically celebrate success at employee events.

A SUCCESSFUL, SUSTAINABLE ORGANIZATION

Investors should be happy as well. The company's stock has risen to about $112 a share in March 2019 from around $79 five years ago, with an annual dividend of about 1%. Revenues and profit margins have consistently increased year to year as well, and costs have been reduced, despite hits in various sectors of its diverse lines of technology business. With these financial results come the comfort of a company that is squarely and positively addressing the environmental, social and governance (ESG) issues that it and a growing number of investors, customers and employees believe are the foundation of a successful and sustainable organization.

Because Enterprise Engagement focuses specifically on the social aspects of ESG, below are some highlights of the human capital elements disclosed in Integrated Report that serve as a benchmark for other companies seeking to focus on customer and employee engagement and well-being. SAP has published the Integrated Report (IR) encompassing its full-year financial, social, and environmental performance since 2012, following recommendations from the International Integrated Reporting Framework.

In addition to providing detailed financial results related to revenues, profits and expenses, the IR discloses the number of employees (96,500); personnel expenses per employee, including stock plans ($115,000); number of women working at SAP versus total number of employees (33%); women in management (25%); employee engagement index (84%); business health culture index (78%); leadership trust index (60%); employee retention (94%); and Net Promoter Score, (-5.0 — *note: this is a good score*). With annual sales of $26 billion, the company's revenue per employee is about $269,892. These numbers, both those that are good or in need of improvement, are further addressed in the Integrated Report and include extensive details on the company's workforce and customer engagement strategies, some of which are highlighted below.

THE EMPLOYEE-CUSTOMER CONNECTION

The report addresses the connection between employees and customers that is the foundation of Enterprise Engagement and ISO Quality People Management principles. The report states: "Our people are key to enabling our customers to successfully become intelligent enterprises. For this reason, we strive to understand the needs of today's employee and how a 21st-century organization must evolve to keep attracting, retaining and growing current and future talent. To address these expectations and to provide intelligent, integrated and meaningful experiences for our people, we continuously evolve our Human Resources (HR) strategy."

According to the report: "Our HR strategy details our people implications, derived from the corporate strategy, into areas of strategic investment that span the entire employee lifecycle. At the same time, it allows us to create a culture that deals successfully with the agility and scope of a digital workplace built on our purpose to help the world run better and improve people's lives. This culture inspires innovation, leads change, and ultimately creates employee satisfaction."

This systematic connection of the strategic plan to culture and people is also emblematic of ISO Quality People Management principles aimed at addressing the needs of all key stakeholders. The company report also addresses its customer engagement strategy: "SAP's purpose is to help the world run better and improve people's lives. We achieve this by providing solutions that help our customers tackle the challenges of today's world to be successful. We can only do this with a sharp focus on our customers' needs. We want our customers to see a company that listens and responds to their needs. We want to design and develop with their needs in mind. We want them to experience a constantly improving SAP." The report explains the basis for its excellent -5% net promoter score, which includes multiple means of gaining ongoing feedback from customers.

The current strategy also includes "Harmonizing our interactions with customers. Continuing to evolve our portfolio into a seamless intelligent enterprise offering. Further integrating customer experience for our cloud assets in particular. We engage in this process transparently, as we believe transparency leads to accountability." SAP says it's basing its strategy in part on its belief that the world is moving towards an "experience economy."

BUSINESS ADVICE FROM McDERMOTT

Below is a sampling of both business and personal advice from McDermott for other CEOs or aspiring CEOs.

- **Engage employees.** "If a vision is not supported by the workforce, even the most brilliant ideas risk being nothing more than light bulbs in a basket." From his book *Winners Dream: A Journey from Corner Store to Corner Office*.

- **Forever be the underdog.** "I have no interest in mediocrity or maintaining the status quo, even if they're safer bets," he told CNBC. "I love that I was and still feel endlessly like an underdog. Because it keeps you humble to remember where you came from. And it keeps you hungry because if you stopped thinking like an underdog, anything you have achieved can and will be taken away from you if you neglect your responsibility to keep it."

- **Address the why.** McDermott's LinkedIn page notes that "As a leader, you can't simply tell people what they need to do. You need to make sure that everyone on your team understands the vision for where the company is going and why that is where it needs to head. You have to make sure they fully grasp what part they play in making that vision a reality. Your teammates will give you their best effort if they know that what they are doing matters."

- **The need for vision.** "Great leadership needs to be about more than just meeting goals--it has to be about vision."

- **Dignity for all.** "If you are a leader, remember that every team member deserves the dignity of understanding how they can participate in the masterpiece of success."

- **The wealth of diversity.** "A diverse team is the key to success, and anyone not looking to include people from all walks of life is missing a golden opportunity."

- **Trust through tough times.** "When times are tough, trust can decline, but that's when people need to trust one another more than ever. If we want to improve people's lives and make the world run better, trust is a key component to success."

- **Wellness and well-being.** "The physical and mental wellness of our team is paramount. This is one of the many reasons I urge everyone at SAP to do things outside of the office that give them joy. If our people don't take care of their health, ultimately everything else suffers, and I want everyone at SAP to have a dream job. I want people to be happy and to be inspired to have a thrilling career. The people who power this company are the most important part of it."

- **Put people first.** "Do this with your friends, your family, your employees, and even those you don't know. Do everything you can to ensure you make this world a better place for everyone."

PERSONAL ADVICE FROM McDERMOTT

- **"Dreams are meant to be big.** It doesn't matter how impossible something may seem or how slim the chances of it coming true may be."

- **Perseverance.** "Never allow present circumstances to interfere with your original dream. Where you are today does not define who you are and says nothing about where you might be tomorrow."

- **Growth through challenge.** "Every difficult situation we face in our lives is an opportunity to learn and grow. We can extract benefits from whatever hardships we're faced with, if we can only identify what the good in the situation is."

- **Empathy**. "Successful salespeople and respected leaders know how to empathize," McDermott told *Forbes* in 2015. "Whether selling or leading, you must put yourself in other people's shoes, understand their needs, care about what pains them and do all you can to solve their problems."

Honorary CEO Citation for
Quality People Management

Gary Vaynerchuk, CEO, VaynerMedia

The sole purpose of the ISO 10018 Honorary CEO Citation for Quality People Management is to profile CEOs who, through information available from the public record, demonstrate a strategic and systematic approach to engaging all stakeholders as part of their core management principles. Ironically, most of the CEOs with these management principles rarely talk about them, as if they are happy to let their competitors manage their organizations the old-fashioned way: that is, more or less command-and-control, top-down management, with a reactive and ad hoc approach to engaging people, and a poorly defined culture rife with internal silos. For anyone who follows Gary Vaynerchuk, CEO of VaynerMedia, on social media, this CEO makes it his business to share his vision of how to succeed through people to anyone who will listen.

VaynerMedia is a privately held digital media company that is part of Vaynerchuk's Vayner X holding company that has stakes in multiple businesses. Founded in 2009, VaynerMedia has grown rapidly to over 800 employees, with many well-known accounts. In our evaluation, the company had two strikes against it, unimpressive Glassdoor.com scores and the lack of any way to contact a human by telephone.

Some might ask why the ISO 10018 Honorary CEO Citation could go to a CEO with poor scores on Glassdoor.com—only 36% would recommend a friend to work there and only 48% rank Vaynerchuk highly. First, Glassdoor.com is only one of about 10 criteria we use to select CEO candidates, since there are so many specific reasons why one company or CEO would get rankings different from another and because the self-selecting survey methodology used by Glassdoor is not considered a scientific assessment of actual sentiments at a given organization. The second reason is that the purpose of the ISO 10018 CEO Citation is to highlight CEOs with a clear, documentable track-record of having a strategic and systematic approach to engaging all stakeholders—not to suggest that this CEO is perfect or that people management systems are the only determining factor of success. Yes, people are critical to success, but organizations can run into many unforeseen economic, competitive, or growth life-cycle issues that can strain the beams of the ship to a near breaking point, despite a CEO's best intentions. Also, while a focus on people is a competitive advantage, the ability to succeed, at least in the short term, without great leadership skills explains why so many CEOs see no need to have a strategic and systematic approach to engaging all stakeholders.

As to the inability to find a human at a company that's supposed to be the essence of being human, this cannot be a disqualifying oversight at a business-to-business media company with a semi-celebrity CEO who many people want to contact, not to mention probably thousands of companies that want to sell him and his company media and other services.

A PUBLIC COMMITMENT TO PEOPLE

We have selected Gary Vaynerchuk because almost no CEO anywhere is more out-front and willing to share his or her strategic focus on customers, employees, and communities. Unlike most CEOs, who remain below the social media radar, Vaynerchuk is a social media firehose of content across almost every social media platform and format—written, video, face-to-face, infographics, animation, etc. In fact, unless one enjoys the super-high energy, arms-flailing, torrent-of-talk approach New York City residents live with every day, Vaynerchuk's social media (and perhaps personal) presence might be overwhelming or even off-putting to some with a calmer nature. Given that most CEOs take the exact opposite approach in terms of public advocacy for putting people first, we give Vaynerchuk extra credit for his strategy of making his focus on helping people the fundamental essence of his brand strategy. His posts are filled with free advice. On top of that, Vaynerchuk is among the few in the advertising field who ever even talk about employees. Although his company does not have a brand engagement practice to help his clients foster internal engagement, Vaynerchuk makes employee engagement a regular part of his story.

CEOs are selected for the ISO 10018 Honorary CEO Citation for Quality People Management based on how well their publicly verifiable actions or statements align with the basic principles of the ISO standards and Enterprise Engagement: having a strategic and systematic approach to engaging all stakeholders in a common brand mission. Here is what we found about Vaynerchuk that warrants this ISO 10018 Honorary CEO Citation.

VAYNERMEDIA MANAGEMENT PRINCIPLES

Track record. Success is not the only criteria for selection of this honorary ISO 10018 CEO citation, but it doesn't hurt. Vaynerchuk's story of serial entrepreneurship starting in his childhood is well known to those who follow him, and wine lovers admire him for having turned a small family business into a $60 million e-commerce retailer known as Wine Library at WineLibrary.com. In 2009, Vaynerchuck and his younger brother founded VaynerMedia, which by scoring early clients such as the New York Jets and the NHL, grew rapidly so that it now represents leading consumer, beverage, and other nationally known accounts, employing over 800 people who will be working in the company's new offices in New York City's recently opened eye-popping Hudson Yards complex.

The importance of strategy. Vaynerchuk's social media presence suggests a rapid-fire approach to business, but Vaynerchuk regularly addresses the importance of strategy. "The strategy and smarts I put into my businesses every day are not something that I talk about enough with my community. I disproportionately give credit to the 17-hour work days, when working smart in those 17 hours is just as important. When I didn't even own a computer, why did I want to launch one of the first ecommerce websites? Why did I consciously decide not to make a catalog when everyone else was doing direct mail? Why did I give email marketing all my attention when it was barely a blip on the radar? And what about maybe the most important decision I made for my career: Why did I decide to jump on YouTube and start a wine review show when no one was really producing YouTube shows? All these things involved hard work, obviously. But the hard work was the byproduct of the full commitment to smart strategy. I don't pay attention to what my competitors or peers are doing, because I trust my own smarts and intuition one-trillion percent. I hustle 24/7/365 because I know that what I'm executing against is what will work for me and businesses in the current marketplace. The game plan will work as long as I put in the work."

A focus on culture. In multiple articles and blog posts, Vaynerchuk talks repeatedly about company culture. In an interview with CNBC, he said, "Great company culture isn't about having free snacks in your cafeteria or a foosball table...You build culture by actually talking to people, one by one, and understanding what they care about. It all comes down to being emotionally intelligent. If a CEO tells people he cares about them, for example, but then looks the other way when certain employees are mean to everyone, he's basically sending the message that he doesn't care about how the rest of his employees feel." The CNBC interviewer observes, "If Vaynerchuk is right, and we're heading full speed into an era where the 'human element' is our most important resource, then his advice extends to those beyond CEOs and business owners. No matter what age you are or what demographic cohort you're in, emotional intelligence is the one skill to master if you want to be successful."

On authentic people-centric leadership. Explaining the agency's "people first" focus, Vaynerchuk writes, "A big part of being a leader is being the bigger person – in every situation. It means giving even when you don't get anything in return sometimes. It means taking ownership and accepting blame. You can't simply impose your will because you're now the boss. There will be plenty of times when you will need to swallow your pride and do what's in the best interest of the team. This means empowering those around you to do their jobs, but it also means something else: you need to be able to accept that certain things are your fault. At the end of the day, you're the one leading the charge, so you need to be willing to accept responsibility for your successes, and more importantly, your failures. It all falls on you. No one likes a boss that passes the buck to an employee in a tough situation. If you take the blame, your people will know that you've got their back – no matter what the situation is."

The role of emotional intelligence. Vaynerchuk writes, "Luckily, through social media and the internet...You can create and distribute content, you can search employees by title or name, you can identify customers by geo-location, or individuals who like products that fit your niche. All the information is there, you just have to go online and figure it out. I'm as bullish as anybody on AI and CRM (customer relationship management) and message bots but those things are only going to put you on third base. It's your emotional intelligence and tact and unscalable human effort that takes you home."

Lead from behind. "Most new managers think that becoming a manager is the 'graduation.' Truth is, it's the reverse. Leaders work for their employees... I genuinely believe that the best leadership qualities are maternal, not paternal. It's a lot more appropriate and helpful to have a caring, empathetic, understanding personality when you're a leader than something stern, paternal, or aggressive."

Recruitment. "Jerks destroy culture. Emotional intelligence matters above everything else. Then, I care about the actual tangible skills candidates have. It's not even close. If someone's a jerk, I won't hire him or her – even if their numbers are phenomenal. It's similar to sports – a team that sticks together will end up beating a team of superstars that were put together for one season (over the long term)....Another big piece of advice I give is hiring people that complement your strengths. If you're a visionary type of person, hire someone who is obsessed with Excel (spreadsheets) and freaks out if you're a minute late. Hire someone who loves details. A lot of leaders get caught because they hire friends that are similar to them but aren't what they actually need."

The ROI of nice. "Truth is, you could have the greatest HR tools and software of all time to monitor how your employees are doing – but if you don't actually care about your people at a deep level, you will lose. None of those tools are going to do anything. As a leader, it's my job to give my employees 51% of the value in the relationship. But I'm not Mother Teresa. It's just not practical. If you're using negativity as a way to extract value from employees or people on your team, they'll build resentment towards you and it'll kill your culture long term. I want to create a conversation around the practicality of positivity, kindness, and empathy within my organization. I'm not just saying it to be ideological — instilling those characteristics and traits as part of your culture has significant long-term impact for your business."

Vaynerchuk writes, "Most people who say that kindness is a weakness are giving with expectation. When your kindness is loaded with an ask on the back end, people can smell it from a mile away. You're not actually being nice, you're just using kindness as a disguise to get what you want from the relationship. If you give with a hidden agenda, your kindness will feel fake — and people will notice...When you give without expectation, you're happy no matter what. You can't be taken advantage of because you're playing a different game. Even if I provide all the value in the relationship and I get nothing back in the short term, the worst-case scenario is that I had a positive impact on somebody through my actions. As a human being, that makes me feel really good."

THE ROLE OF HR AT VAYNERMEDIA

At VaynerMedia, Claude Silver, the company's Chief Heart Officer, is No. 2 on the organization chart. "And if there's ever a debate on what's good for our employees vs. what's good for our bottom line, she'll win that debate nine times out of ten," says Vaynerchuk. In an article about her role, Silver writes: "The branding of HR is a lot worse than we'd like it to be. It's why I rebranded our department name from HR to People and Experience team. Culture is a texture. It's a vibe. It's a feel. To me, good culture means spreading kindness. It's about connection, people caring about one another. It's about people having self-awareness, so they care about other people as well. In a nutshell, culture is the heartbeat of a company. It's something that lights up the entire system. If a company has great culture, it can be the backbone of their success. At VaynerMedia, the Chief Heart Officer role was created to scale Gary (Vaynerchuk.) As a very gifted salesperson, he's always in demand. Whether meeting with the head of Toyota, PepsiCo, or giving a keynote speech, or releasing a new book, his time is incredibly valuable. He needed someone else who could help him touch our employees. And to do that, he needed to find someone who shared the same language, had the same beliefs in people, someone who could 'cut through the BS' but came from a place of empathy."

A holistic approach. Asked about her role in HR in an interview with Recruiting Social, Silver says "I'm not just looking at people. I'm not just looking at benefits. I'm not just looking at recruiting. I'm not just looking at, quote-unquote 'HR.' I'm looking at all of that: as Chief Heart

Officer. I'm Chief People Officer, Chief Talent Officer, Chief Culture Officer, Chief Inspiration Officer all together. It's holistic."

Assessment and surveys. Silver writes, "It's my job to have a pulse on what every individual needs at our company. I need to know who needs to have a chat, who needs mentorship, who needs a team change, or anything else. When we have a glitch — even if it's just a tiny blip, like someone having a bad day or a squabble with someone on their team — I want to know. It's why I'm constantly reaching out and touching people, one-on-one, by text message, by emails, on quick phone calls. My days are normally made up of 15-20 one-on-one meetings. And by the time I get to the office at 9 am, I will probably have already sent out just as many texts so people know I'm thinking about them. I meet every single employee to help them remove their own roadblocks that they have in their own heads. I help them lean into their strengths, instead of getting bogged down by their weaknesses. The wonderful thing about managing the problems of 600+ employees is, human beings are very much alike. Even if you and I grew up differently, we both share a lot of the same concerns. We fundamentally have similar desires, fears, limiting beliefs, imposter syndromes, and more. At the core, the human experience is similar for all of us.

"So when I meet with employees, I listen to people with a non-judgmental ear. I collect information and I look for patterns, When I see patterns in specific departments or demographics within the company, I can go and confront these issues at scale...Some companies try to replace one-on-one interaction with surveys. We do use some surveys — I can send out email surveys or polls whenever I want. But if I'm sitting in the same room as you, I'm just going to get so much more by reading your body language and having some warmth and tenderness in the conversation."

Professional development. According to Chief Heart Officer Silver, "Here, you can architect your own career to a large degree. Of course, we all have jobs that need to be done, but since we don't practice micromanagement, people can do more than they'd do at a 'normal' job. Our open office and extensive cross-collaboration between departments helps a lot with that...My mission is to allow people to 'bring their whole selves' to work. When I sit down with people and have conversations on a day-to-day basis, it's not all rainbows and sunshine. I'm dealing with people and life on life's terms. There are a lot of things that happen in life, including some really hard things like personal tragedies. I have to remember that when I'm talking to people about their performance, their day, their purpose, or their achievements, it all has some kind of real life thrown into it. They're thinking about their grandmother when they're talking to me, or their friend who went through a tragedy."

Well-being. Explains Silver, "My wish is not for people to 'compartmentalize' their lives and leave their personal lives at home when they show up for work. My wish is for people to be real here, and for me to be real here. That means I need to bring my whole self to work. I need to show up as I am when I'm not at work. Another way to do this is by helping people develop more self-awareness and understanding of who they are in my one-on-ones. I'll take people through a map of themselves, starting with a question like, 'how does the team see you? What is the value you bring to the team?' We'll go through what they think their value is. If I have feedback to give them, that's a perfect time for me to give feedback. When they say to me, for example, 'I'm strategic' — I'll ask them, 'what does 'strategic' mean?' If they say, 'I'm a problem solver,' I'll follow up with what I think being a problem solver at VaynerMedia means. If I make it my focus to understand what our people want, help them uncover who they are and what their strengths are, and then help them lean into those strengths, I know we'll maintain great culture at VaynerMedia."

How to put people first during rapid growth. "One of the biggest priorities for me is creating a space where people feel physically and emotionally safe," she tells Recruiting Social. "So I'm always ensuring that individuals bring their whole self to work. We want people to come in as quirky as they are, and we want them to feel secure, confident, and amazing. How do you make someone feel secure? How do you make a stranger feel secure? By connecting with them and treating them like they're your friend. And without a doubt, that's one of the emphasis points that Gary (Vayerchuk) and I propagate."

Innovation. "We try to make it so that creativity and ideas can come from everywhere. Someone on the finance team could have an idea for the next Mountain Dew campaign. Someone on the IT team could have an idea on how to improve our operations," says Silver.

What to do with poor performers. Vaynerchuk advises, "There are different types of employees that you'll have to deal with as a manager—underperforming employees that have strong talent, hardworking employees that aren't talented, and more. The way I deal with them is strong communication…When you have the luxury of being the 'judge and the jury' as a manager, the pressure and the onus is on you. If there are employees at VaynerMedia that are highly talented but underperforming, it's my fault for not creating the infrastructure for them to shine."

Confronting siloes and office politics. Writes Silver, "You can't lead with ego at VaynerMedia. There's no place for that at this company. Instead...we instill empathy and kindness among our people. We want to help employees understand what other departments are going through. For example, account managers need to have empathy for what creatives are experiencing day to day. Like, how would a creative feel when their work is being subjectively criticized by a stranger? How would they feel when they're pressured to be creative on a tight deadline? Same thing applies the other way around. What kind of pressure does an account manager face from clients? What kind of tradeoffs do they have to make?"

Recognition. "Spreading empathy really isn't that difficult at an organization," writes Silver, "especially when you have full autonomy to do it. Gary has given me full freedom on this, which definitely helps. One way I do this is by finding and showcasing 'culture champions.' Culture champions are employees who are really bought into what we're doing here and live by our values. Another way I do it is by meeting with every employee one on one."

Community. In her interview with Recruiting Social, Silver says, "So, how do you treat a stranger like a friend? You say hello to them. You organize cultural activities; from Wine Wednesday, to company kickball to Gay Pride mixers. You encourage Slack channels to be created for all communities that are interested; we have 160 Slack channels, around fitness, music, Pride, women, African Americans, The Bachelor, beer, bicycles, and VaynerMedia wellness. There's even a Slack channel called #Vaynerds. And you know what the members do? On Thursday nights, they play Dungeons & Dragons here. I just found that out – that was music to me!"

VAYNERCHUK'S ADVICE FOR CEOs

The importance of saying yes. "As a leader, I'm very yes-minded. I say yes to virtually everything. I say yes to everything because I look at business as a net-net game. Let's say I say yes to 12 things, and seven succeed. On one side, I won seven times. On the other side, I have to deal with failures — including trying to make up for them because I may have let people down directly or indirectly through those losses.

Even if it breaks down into those two categories, I will still take the seven wins that resulted from saying yes to everything rather than just trying to do two or three with the goal of getting them right."

Give trust easily. "I give trust a lot easier than most CEOs would. I think it's just smart. It's offense. The reason most people don't give trust is because they fear losses. They're afraid of an employee messing up, failing, or creating short-term losses in business. But the truth is, at some point, you have to let your kid swim. You have to let your kid swing the bat. And for me, I'd rather do that sooner than later...It blows me away how many managers spend time trying to hire the 'right person' — then micromanage them. Here's how I think about management at work: 1. Don't make people earn your trust — give trust up front, then take it away later if necessary. 2. Don't get confused between legitimate criticism and your own subjective opinion about your employee's creative output. 3. Letting people 'roam free' and expose themselves is the ultimate version of 'scale' — and you need to be unafraid of losses in the short term to be able to achieve that."

The impact of authentic content in marketing. "A lot of people make this mistake when they run ads on social media or create content: They go for the 'ask' in the same piece of content where they're giving value. When you do that, you lose equity and brand with the end consumer."

**Honorary CEO Citation for
Quality People Management**

Colleen Wegman, CEO, Wegmans

There's a lot of talk today about the importance of the employee experience, but let's face it: how do you create a great employee experience for many of the employees that work in the grocery trade, in the kitchens, aisles, butcher departments, checkout counters, etc.? It's tough work no matter how you try to sugarcoat it, often done on weekends, evenings and holidays. This makes Colleen Wegman an easy choice for our ISO 10018 Honorary CEO Citation for Quality People Management. Wegman is President and CEO of this family-owned supermarket chain with a stellar reputation with customers, employees and communities—the natural outcome of an enterprise approach to engagement.

Even though privately held and required to share little information about its business practices, Wegmans clearly demonstrates the case of a CEO-led strategic and systematic approach to engagement that is apparent with a thorough a visit to its stores, website, history, customer and employee ratings, and media coverage. One simple mathematical calculation from numbers supplied on the company's website tells an impressive story: With $8.9 billion in sales and 49,000 employees, the company generates an impressive $181,632 in revenue-per-employee. By comparison, SAP, a technology company with annual sales of $26 billion, has average revenue-per-employee of $270,000. That's an impressive figure when one considers that the average household spends over $7,000 on groceries a year, according to 2015 Bureau of Labor Statistics data, compared with an average spend per employee on Information Technology of $13,000 at mid-sized companies, and about $11,000 at large companies.

As described on its website, Wegmans is a regional supermarket chain with 98 stores: 46 in New York, 17 in Pennsylvania, nine in New Jersey, 11 in Virginia, eight in Maryland and six in Massachusetts. It is ranked 31st on the 2017 *Supermarket News* list of the Top 75 Supermarkets based on sales volume. A family-owned company headquartered in Rochester, NY since its founding in 1916, Danny Wegman is Chairman. Robert Wegman, Danny's father, was Chairman until his death in April 2006. Colleen Wegman, one of Danny's daughters, became President and CEO after joining the company in 1991 and working her way up through various departments. Danny's other daughter, Nicole Wegman, is Senior Vice President.

OUTSTANDING ENGAGEMENT SCORES

Wegmans has stellar scores for customer, employee and community engagement. When the company opened its first store in New York City, the *New York Times* wrote glowingly: "Founded in 1916, Wegmans has consistently been ranked the top grocery store in the nation by *Consumer Reports* and the Food Network, and *Forbes* placed it among the top 10 employers in the country. Because of its emphasis on prepared foods, the company offered to create at least twice as many full-time jobs (200), and more total jobs (600) than any of the rivals. In its first two weeks of hiring, the store will interview exclusively from the three housing projects that border the Navy Yard, a community it hopes will be on both sides of the checkout line, said Danny Wegman, the grocer's third-generation chief executive. "People need not just good food, but good jobs. Brooklyn provides an incredible opportunity for both."

On Glassdoor.com, 94% of 2,100 reviewers approve of the CEO, and 84% would recommend the company to a friend. Wegmans gets an overall rating of 4 on a scale of 1-5, with the types of complaints one would expect, especially from part-time workers, about flexibility related to hours. Wegmans was recently ranked No. 1 for corporate reputation among the 100 most visible companies, according to the 2019 Harris Poll Reputation Quotient® (RQ) study. The company's website has a list of awards far too long to list here, but which includes:

- Ethisphere Institute, a leading business ethics think-tank, recognized Wegmans as one of the world's most ethical companies.

- Consumer Reports subscribers rated Wegmans, Trader Joe's, Publix and Fairway tops among 52 of the nation's major grocery stores.

- American Customer Satisfaction Index (ACSI ranked Wegmans highest among supermarkets and it received the highest score across all retail channels.

- National Down Syndrome Congress gave Wegmans the 2012 Employer Award 'for employing individuals with Down syndrome and providing the necessary supports to ensure positive outcomes.'

- Greatist.com an on-line publication devoted to health and fitness, ranked Wegmans No. 9 on its 2013 list of the *46 Healthiest Companies to Work For*.

- The company has ranked No. 1 since 2015 on *Fortune* magazine's list of the 15 Best Workplaces in Retail.

- The National Council on Aging presented Wegmans with its Distinguished Achievement Award for employing senior adults in June 2014.

- Wegmans is on *Forbes* magazine's list of America's Best Employers from 2015 through 2018, when it ranked No. 8.

- *Fortune* named Wegmans to the magazine's 100 Best Companies to Work For list, every year starting in 1998 through 2019. The company ranked 1st in 2005 and ranked No. 3 in 2019.

- Glassdoor included Colleen Wegman on its 2018 Best CEOs List, ranking her No. 9.

- A survey of more than 12,000 consumers nationwide conducted by Market Force Information ranked Wegmans No. 1 America's Favorite Supermarket in June 2018.

At college in Colorado, as told to the Rochester, N.Y. *Democrat and Chronicle* newspaper, Wegman became interested in health and natural food and was encouraged by her father to bring that philosophy to Wegmans. She says she "believed there was a benefit to bringing more natural foods into our stores. This was when our Nature's Marketplace department, and Wegmans food-you-feel-good-about brand, was born. My dad's advice to me at the time was, lead with your heart, do what you believe is right, and things will work out. The culture of our company continues to be: begin with a belief and a passion for something, apply high standards, and then take measured risk to bring it to fruition." She says there were a lot of "questions about whether a natural foods department would work 25 years ago. However, these products and philosophies are playing a significant role at Wegmans today, and are a key part of our mission to help people live healthier, better lives through food."

A STRATEGIC APPROACH

While the company is privately held and doesn't need to disclose any information about its business results or practices, its careers website reads almost like a Sustainability or Integrated Report published by a public company. It includes extensive information on its brand values, culture and strategic approach to engaging customers, employees and communities. It's no surprise that the Wegmans careers website reflects a strategic and systematic approach; after all, Colleen Wegman advises people to have a written plan for any important initiative.

Brand mission and values. The website plainly states the company's mission: "Our primary business is to help make great meals easy so our customers can live healthier and better lives." The headline of the company's consumer website opens with the headline: "We're Here to Help," offering temporary price reductions on "what families use most." Its values are posted clearly on its jobs website.

- We care about the well-being and success of every person.

- High standards are a way of life. We pursue excellence in everything we do.

- We make a difference in every community we serve.

- We respect and listen to our people.

- We empower our people to make decisions that improve their work and benefit our customers and our company.

Connection between customers and employees: "We believe that good people, working toward a common goal, can accomplish anything they set out to do. In this spirit, we set our goal to be the very best at serving the needs of our customers. Every action we take should be made with this in mind. We also believe that we can achieve our goal only if we fulfill the needs of our own people. To our customers and our people, we pledge continuous improvement, and we make the commitment: Every day you get our best."

Culture. "At Wegmans, diversity is a part of our everyday culture, providing success and opportunity for all. Our people choose us because we've created an environment where we live our values every day, we have fun, and our co-workers are like a second family...We truly embody what it means to be a family. Each of our employees— from our cashiers and cooks to our people in the Distribution Centers and Corporate Offices—works together to provide amazing service to all our customers. And with our volunteerism and drive to achieve our mission of helping families live healthier, better lives through food, we build a sense of camaraderie and a genuine bond."

The commitment to people. "In order to fulfill our goal of being the very best at serving the needs of our customers, we need a caring, diverse team. We strive to attract and retain a team of people that reflects the communities in which we do business. Everyone that works at Wegmans brings unique perspectives, backgrounds and experiences that unite to make us stronger."

Recruitment. We know excellence takes many types of contributions to create. That's why we are constantly looking for people with unique perspectives. Our approach is to integrate diversity of thought into everything we do and ensure there is a level playing field for all to success while measuring our progress. By welcoming, encouraging and supporting different viewpoints—47,000 strong—we fuel collaboration, innovation and continuous improvement. We're seeking highly motivated people who share our values, understand our objectives and embrace our culture no matter their background. By hiring the best, we're able to bring the best to our customers."

Feedback. "At Wegmans, we understand it's not enough to say we empower our employees; it's that we listen to their feedback, and truly care about the success of each person we employ...Employees are empowered to make decisions that improve their work and benefit our company. We invest in various programs to put our employees' ideas into action. Open Door Days, Huddles, Focus Groups, a two-way Q&A blog with our senior vice president of operations are all examples of our commitment to listen to our people closest to the work and closest to the customer to help us continuously improve. We believe this makes our work more fun and more meaningful, whether a cashier, chef, accountant or baker."

Career development. "We invest more than $50 million each year to provide training and development opportunities for our people. Learning at Wegmans includes: department universities, online training, workshops, Dale Carnegie, on-the-job experiences, food rallies, cooking technique certifications, merchandising shows, traveling to supplier partners, and talent development programs like internships, management trainee and leadership development programs. Last year, 25% of our employees received a promotional or lateral learning assignment, which equates to 12,198 people taking on new opportunities via our internal job posting program." Do the math and the company spends an average of $10,000 per full-time employee a year on training and development.

Diversity. "We believe that diversity inspires new ways of thinking and innovation. The Wegmans family believes that the starting point for our diversity and inclusion efforts is our value of Respect. By listening to others' perspectives and respecting each other's talents, we all have an opportunity to learn. Danny Wegman, Chairman, regularly reminds us that when we take time to authentically discover what our people love to do, we can help each other succeed. We have rich diversity inherent in our business: of customers, food cultures, employee roles and professions, various families and lifestyles, nearly 50 different languages spoken, ages spanning from 15 to 96, with a myriad of personalities from all walks of life. We embrace our diversity as a key strength, and we practice inclusion as a key strategy to remain successful for the next 100 years."

Job Design: "We provide cross-training, lateral learning opportunities, mentors and leadership development programs to support every level of your career."

Work/life balance. "Flex scheduling and work/life balance are top reasons people come to work and stay at Wegmans. Store locations have more than 500 employees across 30 departments, allowing our 24/7 operation tremendous flexibility to accommodate changes for student schedules, caring for a sick family member, and personal activities or obligations. We are a family company who wants you to have a healthy work/life balance so you can be your best."

Benefits. "At Wegmans, we believe that if we take care of our people, they'll take care of our customers. That's why we offer more than benefits. We offer you total rewards. This means that you'll get more than health coverage and more than vacation days. As part of the Wegmans family, you'll have a package that covers your health, your well-being, your family and your future." Benefits include:

- Health plans: A choice of a traditional PPO plan with low deductibles or a plan with a lower weekly cost.
- Pre-tax spending accounts; dental coverage that covers cleanings, fillings, crowns and braces.
- Paid vacation time along with six paid holidays a year for eligible employees.
- Employee assistance programs to help find child care, elder care, legal consultations and financial planning.
- Adoption assistance and dependent care savings accounts.
- A commitment to helping people live healthier, better lives starts with our employees: screenings and coaching from our pharmacists and healthy eating tips from Wegmans Registered Dieticians.
- Support for "get moving" activities, customized yoga programs, subsidized Weight Watchers at Work meetings, and employee fitness discounts help you be the healthiest version of yourself while inspiring others.
- Pay: a commitment to making sure starting pay rates are equal to or greater than those of our competitors; premium pay above the base rate for hourly employees who work on a Sunday or a recognized holiday.
- Regular, scheduled pay increases.
- Development programs to build both careers and earning potential.
- A 401(k) plan that matches 50% of the employee's contribution, on up to the first 6% of pay that is saved.
- Discounts on mobile phone service, computers, and tickets to movies and amusement parks, and a corporate perks discount program for a wide range of other products.

Community. "One of our most important values is making a difference in every community we serve. At Wegmans, we're committed to improving the lives of our customers and employees in every way we can. Our focus is on areas in which we feel we can be the most effective. These include:

- Providing food for the hungry
- Promoting healthy eating and active lifestyles
- Enriching the communities in which we have stores
- Supporting programs focused on youth
- Engaging in a company-wide United Way campaign
- Making corporate contributions to support many diverse non-profit organizations in our communities."

In 2018, Wegmans says it donated about 14.5 million pounds of food to local food banks and programs that feed the hungry.

ADVICE FROM COLLEEN WEGMAN

Colleen Wegman hasn't published a book, nor does she appear to seek publicity and is mostly focused on carrying out the mission of the organization. Over the years she has shared some personal reflections based on the company's strong family values. She told the *Rochester Democrat and Chronicle*: "We all grew up in the company...You watch somebody doing something that they love and that inspires you and encourages you to want to be part of that, too. It gets in your blood and becomes part of who you are, the culture. We got to learn about the values of the company that way, and that became instilled in us as well."

Asked why the company pressed on with its investments after the Great Recession, she told the *Rochester Business Journal*: "As a community stakeholder, you feel a responsibility to do more, not less. Our people are feeling it, our customers are feeling it, and so we need to step up, not step aside. We've had to learn how to do that—we've had to make changes as a business. We've had to give more help, not less."

Among other key principles she shared:
- "Always help others. If you do that, you're on your way!"
- "Follow your heart, and doing what you believe is right, every day. If you can, do what you love. It will always bring out the best in you. It sometimes takes some trial and error to get there; however, if you pursue being great at something you love, you have the best chance for happiness, and therefore success."
- "The third principle is to listen, and to take action on what you learn....It's not important to have all the answers yourself.

However, it is important to involve others to come up with the best answers, and it becomes more enjoyable for everyone along the way."

- Do "what you believe is right. Even when it may not look so good short term, it usually pays off in the long run. With our mission of helping people live healthier, better lives, we felt uncomfortable selling cigarettes, as we did so profitably many years ago now. In the year 2008…we decided to eliminate them from our mix and put all our effort into smoking cessation programs for our people. The short-term impact to profit was significant; however, the long-term loyalty impact from both our people, and our customers, ended up being even more significant."

- "As you face challenges in life, remember your own guiding principles. We believe if you lead with your heart, continue to do what you believe is right, every day, it will lead you to great places."

Chapter 7

A CEO's Enterprise Engagement Toolkit

Once a CEO has decided to lead a strategic and systematic approach to engaging all stakeholders, there will be no difficulty finding solution-providers to help with the inter-related components of Enterprise Engagement outlined in this article. The challenge is finding the right combination of tactics and solution-providers who understand the principles of Enterprise Engagement — i.e., the need to strategically and systematically align all the audiences and engagement tactics in a proactive, measurable way rather than the current re-active, siloed manner in which HR, marketing, sales and outside solution-providers battle it out for resources and often fail to cooperate.

The Enterprise Engagement Toolkit

Most organizations already do many of these things but in an ad hoc manner.

» Culture, brand and quality definition.
» Audience recruitment and assessment
» Engagement business plan design
» Leadership coaching
» Communications in all of its forms
   (Digital, video, face to face, print,
   promotional products)
» Learning

» Loyalty
» Promotions, gamification
» Innovation and collaboration
» Job design, diversity
» Rewards and Recognition
» Measurement and analytics
» Enterprise Engagement Portal
   Technology

When looking at the engagement field, it helps to view it in the same way as advertising: there are companies that help lead the management of all elements of the brand architecture, marketing strategies and implementation across platforms, often outsourcing specific elements to other divisions or third-parties, and there are many tactical solution-providers that can help with specific elements of an engagement strategy. In either case, it is essential to have someone and/or an organization at the helm of a strategic, systematic process to ensure that all the tactics move together, and to work with tactical solution-providers who understand the concept of Enterprise Engagement and how their solution supports others to achieve the overall goal.

The fundamental reason for failure to profit from engagement is the lack of a strategic and systematic CEO-led focus on engaging all stakeholders in a measurable way. Such CEOs, at larger organizations at least, can benefit from having a Chief Engagement Officer to lead the effort to engage not just employees but all stakeholders so that all hands are on deck to accomplish organizational goals consistent with the brand and culture.

The engagement solutions covered in this e-book include experts for customer, employee, distribution partner, vendor and community engagement. For complete information on the field, you can purchase Enterprise Engagement: The Roadmap 5th edition, which includes detailed information on the entire field, each tactic, and how they intersect. Here are the specific categories covered in this guide and what organizations need to know about how these services and tactics fit into an overall engagement strategy. You can find a complete directory of Engagement Solution providers at ESM at EnterpriseEngagement.org. Look for the 2019 Directory of Enterprise Engagement Solution providers on the home page.

STRATEGIC SOLUTIONS

- Engagement Agencies help develop, implement and measure a strategic Engagement operating system, which can include managed outsourcing and/or project management.
- Engagement consultants focus on program and process design, development, facilitation and managed outsourcing.

TACTICAL SOLUTIONS

- Branding, Brand Architecture

- Program/Process Design
- Leadership and Culture
- Talent Management
- Surveys, Assessment and Feedback
- Communications
  - Branding/graphics
  - Print
  - Digital
  - Face to face
  - Social
  - Video
- Job design
- Learning
- Incentive Programs
- Loyalty
- Promotions
- Diversity and Community
- Innovation, Collaboration & Empowerment
- Rewards and Recognition
  - Merchandise
  - Gift cards
  - Travel
  - Benefits
- Analytics
- Engagement Technology
- Corporate Sustainability Reporting

WHAT TO LOOK FOR IN STRATEGIC SOLUTION-PROVIDERS

Engagement Agencies

Engagement agencies help develop, implement and measure the strategic plan involving all stakeholders, not just customers or employees. At this point in the evolution of the field, there are but a few of them. A full-service engagement agency assumes complete responsibility for discovery, program design, project management, the specified in-house or managed outsourced services and return-on-investment measurement. These could include any of the above services and more. Unfortunately, unlike in the advertising business, there are very few full-service engagement agencies. It's important to verify their expertise by observing the company's discovery process and verifying expertise and in-house versus outsourced capabilities. An engagement agency consultant should be able to ask insightful questions and make sensible directional recommendations on the fly in a way that can't be faked in sales training. If a recommended solution sounds pat or doesn't ring true, that's a warning sign.

Fees: These companies charge advisory service fees for engagement program design development, project management, managed outsourcing, or services provided in-house, and some may charge fees for points issued and/or redeemed in points-based performance, loyalty, or recognition programs, as well as additional fees for managing any rewards, communications, or other related services provided.

Return-on-investment: Achievement of key scorecard objectives for the organization or particular audience or campaign.

Engagement Consultants

A growing number of individuals or small consulting firms specialize specifically on engagement consulting. Most focus specifically on employee, customer, or channel/sales engagement, but a few are now focusing on an enterprise approach.

Fees: These companies generally charge based on professional services fees for speaking, facilitation and planning.

Return-on-investment: Achievement of key scorecard objectives for the recommended solution.

WHAT TO LOOK FOR IN TACTICAL SOLUTION-PROVIDERS

Branding and Brand Architecture

In the world of Enterprise Engagement, a brand is not just a logo or customer-facing story, it's a 360-degree definition of the values and promises of an organization to all stakeholders. A small but growing number of branding consultants now incorporate this 360-degree view of the brand and include all stakeholders. These companies go beyond creating a graphic image to define the brand's mission, values, personality, organizational culture and the behaviors/actions that support it. An important capability is the ability to employ a process that involves all interested stakeholders and builds a consensus-based rather than top-down solution. Some solution-providers provide survey methods as part of the process to break down barriers to alignment.

Fees: These companies generally charge for professional services, with the deliverable being a clear brand definition developed with the involvement of all interested parties.

Return-on-investment: A brand and culture definition consistent with the organization's organizational strengths and history, and that considers the needs of customers, employees and other stakeholders.

Program/Process Design

A few engagement consultants focus specifically on the design of engagement, incentive, recognition, loyalty and other related types of strategies and tactics. Their capabilities can easily be evaluated by letting them conduct a discovery process. The questions they ask and preliminary observations provided will help you quickly determine the types of insights they can provide. They should be able to talk about a systematic approach and provide a clear return-on-investment model.

Fees: These companies usually charge advisory fees, fees for program management and oversight, and sometimes additional fees for achieving specific goals.

Return-on-investment: Achievement of the desired goals on the scorecard.

Leadership and Culture

A growing number of solution-providers focus specifically on leadership and culture. These firms usually provide speakers, management training and some include assessment and benchmarking or other tools to help address and enhance individual performance management by identifying problem managers. The key to achieving a clear return-on-investment from these services is to ensure they are linked specifically to your brand, mission, values, culture and objectives. The best services provide feedback software that enables your organization to pinpoint individual managers who need attention, with some even providing specific training solutions based on the problem.

Fees: These companies charge for their services on a project or hourly basis, as well as setup and per-seat charges if technology is involved.

Return-on-investment: High talent and net promoter scores.

Recruitment

Today's most effective talent recruitment strategies are based on the "employee brand" established as part of the overall strategic engagement plan. The talent brand is the story your organizations tells prospective employees about the culture, values, rewards and benefits of being part of your organization, as well as information that can help candidates determine if they are the right fit. Some recruitment companies today deploy sophisticated third-party or proprietary testing methods to determine if there's the right cultural fit between a candidate and your company.

Fees: In addition to receiving commissions for recruiting candidates, talent branding companies charge additional fees for assignments to help organizations crystallize a truthful story.

Return-on-investment: Better talent recruitment and higher retention.

Talent Management

Larger or fast-growing organizations can benefit from having a talent management strategy that identifies key skills and personal qualities necessary for each key role on the organizational chart and a succession plan for every key role, as well as a professional development effort within the overall organization to identify candidates for growth and a career development or laddering plan. The deliverable is a clear plan aligned with your brand, culture, values and objectives that is updated on a regular basis according to the size of the organization.

Fees: These companies almost always charge professional services fees.

Return-on-investment: Higher retention, productivity, quality and talent net-promoter scores.

Surveys, Assessment & Feedback

A growing number of technology firms provide employee engagement tools to gauge stakeholder engagement on a regular basis, assess individuals or group performance, attitudes, or actions, or offer platforms that enable stakeholders to provide instant feedback (anonymously, if the organization desires). The key to success with these tools is to make sure the overall survey, assessment and feedback plan is aligned with the strategic plan; that actionable information flows rapidly to the people who need it and can use it; that the process attempts to track the effectiveness of different engagement processes; and that the entire organization knows that the process is taken seriously by the CEO. The best platforms pinpoint management or engagement problem areas with a personalized strategy and tactics to address them.

Fees: Some of these companies charge professional services fees for creation and implementation of surveys and feedback platforms, as well as per-seat charges in some cases. Some also include front-line management and coaching solutions.

Return-on-investment: Critical, real-time and actionable information from all stakeholders can provide an early detection system for a wider problem, identify an opportunity that would have otherwise been overlooked, or pinpoint warning signals and apply solutions before the problem escalates.

Communications

Communications are at the heart of any enterprise approach to engagement, because they provide the platform for aligning the entire organization—customers, employees, distribution partners, vendors, communities, volunteers—anyone who can affect the outcome of your organization. Communications are the equivalent of the "hometown" newspaper that binds a community by sharing its news, services, and by telling the stories of its people in a compelling way.

Content: Organizations can benefit by thinking of themselves as a media company with a strategic communications plan aligned with the overall brand, culture, strategy and objectives to make sure everyone has: 1) a sense of community around the same brand, values, and culture; 2) the information they need about management, markets, products, services and trends that can affect their ability to help external and internal customers; and 3) the specific ways each person can contribute to or benefit from the organizations, no matter what their relationship with it. Organizational communications should be led by people who think like journalists, not marketers, because the goal is to inform, not sell. The most effective communications platform is targeted to each audience—customers, employees, distribution partners, vendors, communities, shareholders, or other constituencies—but are built on the same foundation, either literally, from a technology standpoint in the form of an engagement portal, or in the sense that all communications are aligned so that everyone has similar expectations of the brand.

Media platforms: Having a strategic communications plan helps manage the dizzying array of communications options that can include branding, print, infographics and animation, digital, face-to-face (events), social media, video, and three-dimensional—promotional products and gifts. The key is to leverage the appropriate platforms to support of all your communications in an aligned, integrated fashion, using the "drip-marketing" approach advocated by marketing innovator Seth Godin. Rather than try to use every medium, analyze your audiences and the potential return-on-investment of your communications against your plan to establish the right mix. If your company doesn't have the resources to produce this content in-house, there are many internal and external communications companies that can help develop your strategy and tactical plan, not to mention many eager freelancers laid off from publishing companies. The key is to create an overall story and break it into digestible soundbites over the course of the year in an orchestrated fashion and in a systematic and measurable way, gauging feedback and the popularity of topics all along the way.

Permission management: Consumers are increasingly concerned about their privacy and the number and nature of communications they receive and how they receive them. The larger the organization, and the more it involves consumers, the more it needs a professional permission-management strategy, not only to anticipate coming regulations but to also increase customer receptivity to communications.

Fees: Content marketing companies generally charge professional fees for content creation and production.

Return-on-investment: Higher probability of achieving specific goals; higher levels of stakeholder understanding of the brand, value and goals as measured through surveys or feedback.

Job Design

How to make jobs more interesting, meaningful and flexible is one of the most overlooked ways to not only engage people but to enhance productivity and quality, not to mention employee experience. Job design can enhance engagement by making jobs more interesting and more enriching by enabling people to profit from job-sharing programs that lead to greater work-life flexibility. Outside experts can help analyze your organization's task requirements through employee involvement, observational processes and skill assessments to determine the optimal way to minimize the sorts of rote and mechanical operations that contribute to disengagement, accidents and turnover. In so doing, they can often identify the best ways to create job-sharing opportunities to break up routines and enable people to cover for colleagues to reduce the impact of absences.

Fees: Job design consultants generally charge professional services fees.

Return-on-investment: Higher retention and talent net-promoter scores, and higher internal or external customer service.

Learning

A huge and thriving industry of online and offline learning and gamification companies exist to help companies develop strategic and tactical learning programs to support either an overall Enterprise Engagement strategy or a more focused skills-oriented program. In either case, the key is to make sure that the learning strategy supports the overall brand, values and culture, and is integrated and aligned with other engagement strategies and tactics. Too often, organizations segregate learning from incentive, recognition, or other engagement strategies, missing an enormous opportunity to promote and support the key behaviors and actions necessary for internal and external customer satisfaction.

Fees: Learning companies charge fees for learning program development and for technology, oftentimes on a per-seat basis.

Return-on-investment: Higher levels of internal or external customer satisfaction as measured through engagement surveys, higher retention and net promoter scores.

Incentive Programs

Some estimates put annual spending on incentive programs using non-cash rewards for employees and salespeople at close to $50 billion, with much more spent on cash incentives that go untracked, and yet the latest surveys indicate that only about 25% of companies have a formal return-on-investment strategy for their programs. The most common errors are:

- Rewarding the top 20% of people who would have performed anyway.
- Failing to move the middle-60%.
- Failing to reward both results and the actions that lead to results to ensure that people are achieving their goals in an ethical or sustainable manner — i.e., in the customer's best interest.
- Failing to distinguish between compensation and recognition.
- Fostering competition or lack of cooperation.
- Failing to integrate the incentive program with the organization's assessment, communications, learning, community and other platforms to engage people in an integrated way.

Fees: Many incentive companies charge small fees for technology, program design and project management to make their profits on markups on rewards. This approach has several drawbacks, including:
1. The recipients pay for the consulting and other services used to engage them and often know they are getting a poor value for the points they have earned.
2. The purchasing department doesn't understand why the cost of the products is so high and may discount the value of expertise provided by the solution-provider in program design and implementation.
3. Depending on the program structure, there will be breakage (unredeemed points), for which the client is often paying.

Recommendations: The most appropriate and transparent model involves professional service fees for program design; setup and per-seat charges for technology if involved; payment upon points issuance when participants achieve the goals or perform the desired actions; and payment upon redemption for the awards with the appropriate markup for catalog curation and management, technology, customer service, shipping, tracking and reporting.

Return-on-investment: Few if any engagement or other business tactics have a clearer ROI if properly implemented, using both action and results measures to track the correlation between what happens and what gets achieved.

Loyalty

Of all the areas of engagement undergoing the greatest disruption, the loyalty business is at the top of the list. The industry grew up out of a very transactional, rewards- and points-based approach that focused mostly on carrots. Today, organizations of all sizes have determined that loyalty goes beyond transactional added-value or discounts to include the entire customer experience and emotional connection to the brand, and so have begun to take a more 360-degree approach. This means developing strategies that not only reward people for loyalty but also help create an emotional connection by adding value through information, experiences, special privileges and customer councils, and in doing so achieve a greater, more measurable return-on-investment from the relationship.

Fees: Loyalty companies charge professional service fees for program design and implementation, set up, per-seat or other fees for loyalty technology and fees for rewards, catalogs, redemption management, customer service and shipping.

Return-on-investment: Like incentive programs, loyalty is one of the most measurable of all engagement tactics, as the ability to measure revenue per employee, frequency of purchase and willingness to recommend are relatively easy to track.

Promotions

Sweepstakes and contests remain a viable way to generate attention with all audiences. To achieve the best results, their objectives, theme, message and reward selection are tightly aligned with the overall engagement plan, brand, culture, values and objectives. Note that promotions having to do with consumers often involve an understanding of how to leverage other marketing and social media strategies, as well as negotiate myriad state and some federal statutes depending on the industry, so it's critical to work with an expert.

Fees: Sweepstakes, contest and related gamification companies charge for professional services and legal advisory fees, program set-up, prize selection, redemption, and customer service fees.

Recommendations: If your promotion involves consumers or any critical audience, get expert advice, as what might seem simple and obvious about a promotion to the uninitiated can be a landmine leading to a social media firestorm or worse. The promotion agency's website and history will provide an immediate indication of their depth of experience.

Return-on-investment: Properly designed sweepstakes or contests have very clear measures in terms of eyeballs and engagement that generally can easily be tracked. However, if the underlying product or service offer lacks value, no promotion, however clever, can generate a true return-on-investment.

Diversity and Community

Having a diverse, cohesive community provides a competitive edge because of the range of perspectives contributed when all stakeholders are engaged. Every human capital strategy should include in its employee, distribution partner and customer engagement plan a specific strategy or tactical plan for enhancing diversity. Organizations with an active communications strategy and platform support the organizations of value to their customers and encourage employee clubs or communities to work together to unite people of diverse interests. Every effort should be taken to encourage cooperation between these clubs on joint activities of mutual interest to promote cohesiveness across the organization. Every one of every race, ethnicity, sex, or other orientation shares common values of humanity that can create a unifying theme, bring people together, and make them feel better and more fulfilled.

Fees: Consultants assisting with diversity and community services generally charge professional service fees.

Return-on-investment: Achievement of a representative cross section of communities as employees, customers, distribution partners, vendors, recipients of community support, combined with a high level of retention, net promoter and engagement survey scores.

Innovation, Collaboration & Empowerment

Organizations with a strategic and systematic approach to engaging all stakeholders know that crowd-sourcing ideas from all communities in a meaningful way is a powerful motivator and source of beneficial ideas or problem identifiers. The best ideas can come from customers, employees, distribution partners — anyone, including a young person fresh out of school or someone working in the warehouse. On the other hand, many companies with innovation strategies overlook the importance of engaging the people involved, focusing more on process and technology than on people. While there are a number of companies with sophisticated innovation consulting and technology services, the key is to have the commitment of the CEO and a team to make sure the human element is addressed and that all ideas get reviewed with proper communication, acted upon if appropriate, tracked for return-on-investment, rewarded and communicated. If an idea is rejected, the submitter should know why. For innovation to be self-sustaining, the community needs to know who contributed what and when, the benefit to the organization and how contributors were recognized. The best innovation strategies are built into a collaborative culture that encourages employees to work together in teams to come up with new ways to improve processes, outcomes and experiences.

Fees: Innovation companies usually charge professional service fees and often technology setup and per-seat charges.

Return-on-investment: Innovation is one of the most measurable of all engagement tactics; it is clearly tracked by the value of the ideas implemented.

Rewards and Recognition

In perhaps no area of engagement is more money spent based on the least amount of science. Although there are now dozens of useful studies on the best use of rewards and recognition, most companies fail to follow basic principles identified by years of research and supported by common sense.

Program design: The way a gift, incentive, or recognition program is designed is as important as the reward itself. Great care should be given to make sure that the right behaviors are encouraged and messages sent, and that there are no overlooked or unintended consequences.

The reward experience: It is equally important to distinguish between rewards/recognition and compensation and pricing, and to make sure that the selection of the product, the brand and the personalization and customization of the reward is appropriate and heartfelt, in such a way that it creates a buzz throughout the entire organization. The most effective programs use brands selectively as a medium to tell a story about the company's values and understanding of the recipient or include some kind of memorable experience.

Fees: Many rewards and recognition companies roll their catalog, technology and advisory fees into the reward markup; others might separate out fees for the catalog or advisory fees.

Return-on-investment: Generally, these organizations can be evaluated against the scorecard developed for the program in which they are used—i.e., to promote specific behaviors, actions, or results consistent with the brand, values and objectives. Recipient surveys can be used to track the reward and redemption experience.

Benefits

Over the last few years, many organizations have stepped up their efforts to provide flexible working arrangements, perquisites, discounts on products, health club memberships and other benefits to attract talent. All these programs have sustainable value only if they're part of a CEO-led strategic and systematic approach to engaging all stakeholders. Rarely do perquisites have sufficient value to offset the pernicious effects of indifferent CEOs or managers. Under the best of circumstances, benefits and perquisite programs are designed to align with the brand, culture, values and objectives so that they're consistent with the overall organizational story, brand and culture.

Fees: Business models vary widely depending on the type of perquisite, with some employee discount programs having a very low cost based on the ability of the organization to generate aggregate buying volume.

Return-on-investment: Higher retention and net promoter scores.

Analytics

This may be one of the more misunderstood elements of engagement. Analytics go beyond straightforward data analysis to detect leading indicators and prescriptive solutions based on those indicators. Modern analytics is not about looking backward but using regressive analysis and other techniques to predict the future and/or to run "what-if" scenarios based on actual behavioral data rather than simple surveys. This sounds pernicious but used in the cause of helping create a better employee or customer experience, analytics provide a powerful tool.

For instance, while most companies don't follow these findings, analytics often indicate that the faster a company responds to an upset customer (i.e., the quicker that unhappy person finds a soothing human being), the better the outcome in terms of re-engagement and a greater willingness to recommend.

Fees: These companies charge professional service fees to provide the high-level brainpower and database analysis necessary to come up with actionable, data- and behavior-based recommendations or warnings, as well as recommendations on the most useful data available to achieve actionable results.

Return-on-investment: Recommendations for specific strategies or tactics that can lead to more predictable, positive results or anticipate problems and be tested in the field.

Engagement Technology

Companies seeking to engage an enterprise of customers, employees, distribution partners, vendors and communities can use a wide variety of technology platforms, when the ideal state is to integrate and align engagement across the enterprise in the way achieved by CRM (customer relationship management) technology. The rise of an enterprise approach to engagement has spurned the development of a new category known as Enterprise Engagement Technology that seeks to integrate and align on one platform all the key audiences as well as the key areas of engagement, including assessment, communications, learning, community and diversity, innovation, rewards and recognition, etc. These technologies may or may not be linked to a specific reward system or designed to be linked to any reward solution desired. Some incentive, recognition and loyalty companies have their own proprietary platforms.

Fees: Generally, there are setup and customization charges, as well as per-seat fees and additional costs for rewards, catalog curation, redemption, shipping and customer service. Some companies will charge less for the technology if there is a reward program, and perhaps nothing for the technology if there is enough reward volume. Some companies will not let you use their technology unless there are rewards involved.

Return-on-investment: Enterprise engagement technology has the potential to be the equivalent of customer relationship management

(CRM) for the enterprise that goes beyond tracking relationships to promoting and enabling all the behaviors and actions conducive to organizational success. The resulting measures will be higher revenue per customer and employee and higher talent and customer net promoter scores.

Corporate Sustainability Reporting

Starting in the 2010s, many organizations began to publish corporate responsibility reports mostly touting their accomplishments in the domains of DEI (diversity, equity, and inclusion), community activities, and sometimes information about their policies related to customers and employees. In part to combat increasing practices related to greenwashing, or making misleading claims for marketing purposes only, the European Union passed the Corporate Sustainability Reporting Directive that requires organizations operating in the EU with 250 or more employees, $44 million and sales, and a few other criteria to make detailed disclosures on the risks and opportunities they create for customers, employees, distribution and supply chain partners, communities, and the environment, including about 80 specific metrics. The reports must be submitted digitally in a prescribed format so that they can be made available in a public database. Many attorneys believe the new law will have an impact on international sustainability reporting practices equivalent to the impact of the GDPR (General Data Protection Regulation) on marketing both inside and outside of the EU.

As a result, the traditional approach to corporate responsibility reporting is on its way out to be replaced with corporate sustainability reporting consistent with the framework of European Union law.

Chapter 8

Resources

Here is a general overview of the field and resources available.

ENTERPRISE ENGAGEMENT PRINCIPLES AND TERMS

Applying a CEO-led strategic and systematic approach to engaging all stakeholders provides one of the most sustainable ways to achieve organizational goals, and yet some studies estimate that less than 20% of organizations have a formal ROI plan to manage Human Capital. Here's a quick fact sheet on the field of Enterprise Engagement.

Enterprise Engagement Definition: A strategic and tactical process to achieve organizational results by fostering the proactive involvement of all stakeholders who can contribute to success.

Stakeholder Capitalism Definition: Enhancing returns for investors only by creating value for customers, employees, supply chain and distribution partners, communities and the environment.

ISO Annex SL and ISO 10018 Quality People Management standards. All 60 ISO management standards affecting up to 2 million companies now require a formal, written CEO-led process to engage all stakeholders in the organizational mission and must be able to demonstrate how the plan is implemented at the strategic and tactical level. While an organization is granted great leeway in its journey to certification, it must be able to disclose a strategic and tactical plan addressing all related stakeholders with measurable results. Companies that follow the new ISO 10018 Quality People Management guidelines and use the Enterprise Engagement Operating System (See Chapter 3) will effectively meet the requirements of Annex SL at the same time.

What's New: Enterprise Engagement and the related ISO Annex SL and ISO 10018 standards do for stakeholder engagement what ISO 9001 quality standards and methods such as Six-Sigma have accomplished for manufacturing and logistics: enhance efficiency and improve performance through a strategic, systematic, and auditable approach. The standards require a formal proactive effort led by the CEO and all levels of management, and the company must have a system that connects all the dots between objectives, management, stakeholders, etc., as well as clear strategies, tactics and measures.

Benefits: Greater financial return and share-price performance for public companies through a better experience for customers, employees and all stakeholders; reduced reputation and litigation risks; lower marketing and recruitment costs; greater efficiency; enhanced safety and occupational health; and greater community support.

BRIEF HISTORY OF THE FIELD

1980-2000: Formative Period. Visionaries in quality management and marketing identify the need to authentically address the people issue, including W. Edwards Deming, Peter Drucker, Tom Peters, Leonard Schlesinger and James Heskett, Curt Coffman, Marcus Buckingham and Seth Godin, among others. The University of Luton in the U.K. publishes a study identifying the link between customer and employee engagement.

2002-2008: First Formal Research Institute Founded. The Forum for People Performance Management and Measurement is founded at Northwestern University in 2002, conducting six years of research from 2002 to 2008 that further helps identify the connection between customer and employee engagement and organizational performance.

2005: First National Business Media Reference. The *Harvard Business Review* publishes the ground-breaking article, Manage Your Human Sigma, by Gallup consultants demonstrating a clear link between customer and employee engagement.

2008: Enterprise Engagement Alliance Formed to Create Formal Roadmap and Curriculum. Several dozen corporate practitioners, solution-providers and academics form the Enterprise Engagement Alliance at TheEEA.org to create a formal curriculum on how to implement an enterprise approach to engagement in a measurable way.

2009: First Enterprise Engagement Curriculum Launched at EEA.tmlu.org; First edition of *Enterprise Engagement: The Roadmap* published.

2012: Stock Index Created. The EEA creates the first Engaged Company Stock Index, which has consistently outperformed the S&P 500 and is now tracking 40 percentage points higher than the S&P.

2013: ISO Recognizes the Human Factor. The International Organization for Standardization recognizes that it has overlooked the human factor in standards and publishes Annex SL requirements that now apply to 60 ISO standards, including ISO 45001, along with Quality People Management standards that reflect Enterprise Engagement principles.

2015: First Executive Position. Adobe names an executive in charge of both the Customer and Employee Experience.

2016: Investors Awaken. Investors join forces to promote disclosures of Human Capital investments and outcomes.

2017: First Certification for ISO Annex and ISO 10018 Certification, Investor Pressures Mount. The International Center for Enterprise Engagement at TheICEE.org is formed to create the first formal certification for ISO 10018 Quality People Management, which audits for the fundamental issues of Annex SL and offers a way for companies to promote their commitment to people. Nearly $15.7 trillion in investment capital calls for engagement disclosures in SEC filings.

2018: More Corporations Embrace Human Capital. 200 multinational corporations form the Social and Human Capital Coalition to promote the creation of Human Capital reporting standards. The JUST Capital ETF focused on people raises record $215 billion on its first day.

2019: Annex SL in Full Effect. Starting in 2019, Annex SL will be required at up to 2 million companies, which will now have to demonstrate a formal Human Capital and Enterprise Engagement plan.

2019-2020: The Business Roundtable pronounces a new charter for organizations that addresses the interests of all stakeholders, followed by similar pronouncements in 2020 by the Work Economic Forum at its annual Davos Conference and Larry Fink, CEO of BlackRock, in his annual letters to shareholders.

2021-2023: A business media backlash grows against Stakeholder Capitalism and the related concept of ESG (Environmental, Social, Governance) from the right as a form of corporatism and from the left as greenwashing. Some US states try to pass anti-ESG laws. Meanwhile, the public remains largely unaware of either topic.

ENTERPRISE ENGAGEMENT RESOURCES

Overall Information

TheEEA.org offers complete information on the field, Enterprise Engagement services and the Engaged Company Stock Index.

Free eBooks

The Enterprise Engagement Alliance provides eBooks on a growing number of engagement topics, including:

Enterprise Engagement and ISO Standards: A guide to ISO Annex SL and related standards. See EnterpriseEngagement.org.

Free News and Information

Go to **ESM** at **EnterpriseEngagement.org** for extensive information and free newsletters, or follow us on our social media platforms.

2019 Enterprise Engagement Solution-Provider Directory at **EnterpriseEngagement.org**.

Go the ESM library for a comprehensive collection of links to resources in all aspects of stakeholder management.

Free Tools

The Enterprise Engagement Benchmark Indicator enables companies to measure their engagement strategies against best practices. The ROI of Engagement Calculator demonstrates the return-on-investment of improving your company's employee engagement scores. **Go to: http://www.theeea.org/resources/benchmark-tools/**

Online and Live Learning

The Enterprise Engagement Academy at the TheEEA.org provides a comprehensive education and certification program on implementation and provides customized training on implementation, measurement, and corporate sustainability reporting.

Textbook

Enterprise Engagement: The Roadmap, 5th Edition **- How to Achieve Organizational Results Through People and Qualify for ISO 10018 Certification**.

Available at Amazon.com and BarnesAndNoble.com. This is the first and most comprehensive book on Enterprise Engagement and the new ISO Annex SL and ISO 10018 Quality People Management standards.

Free Course Syllabus

A syllabus that instructors can use for a single class, a week, or full semester course on Enterprise Engagement. (*See http://www.theeea.org/ learning/engagement-course-syllabus/*)

ISO 10018 Certification and Learning

The International Center for Enterprise Engagement at TheICEE.org has created the first formal certification program for ISO 10018 Quality People Management, as well as a learning program that is free to active professors and instructors. There is a paid three-hour web or on-location training program available that includes preparation for EEA certifications and other useful information for solution providers and organizations. (See TheICEE.org/events for options.)

Enterprise Engagement Consulting and Professional Services for Corporations and Other Organizations

The EEA's Engagement Agency consulting firm provides multiple services for any organization seeking to profit from the field of Enterprise Engagement and new ISO Annex SL and ISO 10018 Quality People Management standards. Services include: 1) Human Capital and Enterprise Engagement client audits. 2) Enterprise Engagement strategic or tactical plan design. 3) Enterprise Engagement plan oversight or implementation. 4) Enterprise Engagement support. 5) Creation of Sustainability and Integrated Reports. 6) Implementation of or training on the Enterprise Engagement Operating System. 7) Assistance with training and business development for solution providers.

For Information, contact: Bruce Bolger at 914-591-7600, ext. 230; Bolger@TheEEA.org.

About the Author

Bruce Bolger is founder of the Enterprise Engagement Alliance (EEA) at TheEEA.org, an outreach and education organization, and of the International Center for Enterprise Engagement (ICEE) at TheICEE.org, which provides the first certification program for ISO 10018 Quality People Management.

Bolger knew something was wrong with management his first year out of college as a junior editor at a highly regimented trade association publishing group. He started experiencing the challenges of leadership as a young Publisher of a trade publication covering the airline industry, and later learned what it was like to be an executive for a highly successful employee-owned company whose CEO sincerely cared about people and had a strategic and systematic approach to engaging all stakeholders, and he saw what happened when the company was sold to a private equity firm that drained it of its soul until it was literally no more.

Bolger founded the Center for People Performance Management and Measurement at the Medill School of Integrated Marketing at Northwestern University in the early 2000s to conduct academic research on the connection between human capital and financial performance and, based on the research findings of that and other organizations, the Enterprise Engagement Alliance at TheEEA.org was founded in 2008 to create the first education and outreach program on this new field. Similarly, the International Center for Enterprise Engagement was created in late 2017 to enable organizations to put Enterprise Engagement into action through the application of ISO 10018 Quality People Management standards.

The author writes and speaks frequently on all aspects of Enterprise Engagement and ISO Human Resources standards. He is co-author of *Enterprise Engagement: The Roadmap*, now in its 5th edition, and he co-authored the original Fodor's *Short Escapes* experiential book series, now online at Shortescapes.net, as well as the Frommer's *Best Beach Vacation* series, no longer in print.